The Girl From The Forgotten Village

MARY ROSE RAFFAELE-SCALA

Order this book online at www.trafford.com
or email orders@trafford.com

Most Trafford titles are also available at major online book retailers.

Printed in the United States of America.

ISBN: 978-1-4669-9946-6 (sc)
ISBN: 978-1-4669-9928-2 (e)

Trafford rev. 09/05/2013

 www.trafford.com

North America & international
toll-free: 1 888 232 4444 (USA & Canada)
fax: 812 355 4082

PART 1

CHAPTER 1

Although their had been a promise of spring in the air, March 13,1935, was a parody for it. It had been snowing lightly the day before. Raffaela was beginning to feel contractions. She had hoped the weather would hold out until at least after her baby was born. By six o/clock in the evening, overseen inches of snow had fallen. The contractions were becoming more prominent. Raffaela knew her child would arrive before the next dawn. Bruno attempted to drive his model 'T' to the next village of Kinzua to summon  Dr. Flat. That proved fatal. The 'T' was stuck in a snow bank a short distance from the house. One of the neighbor men was

 already putting his boots on to go. He walked six miles in frigid weather with snow belting him all the way .... Three hours later he had returned with Dr. Flat in the horse and buggy.

Little Maria did not wait for the doctor. Two of her great

aunts, Censa and Jamila delivered her. They were known to be the village midwives, but Bruno wanted Dr. Flat there to make

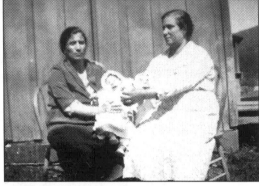

sure all would be well. Raffaela was a very frail; a small women that was beyond her child bearing years. Maria said hello to her world at 3:15 a.m., March 14th, 1935. Maria Rosina Raffaele's birth certificate stated she was

born in Morrison, Pa., McLean County, Hamilton Township, and is a U S citizen. 'Raffaela and Francesco, the first child, had come to this small village in the summer of 1932. Bruno' like the rest of the men, had made several trips back and forth from Italy for several years. Each summoned their families one at a time as they became financially secure enough and were assured of housing and a job.

Raffaela and Frank

Frank arrived in Kane at 8:00 a.m. on a Monday morning. Bruno was to meet them in a couple of hours. When he didn't show up by ten o'clock, Raffaela became very worried. After speaking with the attendant at the terminal, he suggested that a friend of his could drive them the short distance to

Morrison for a few dollars. Then two miles from the terminal, they spotted Bruno coming the other way. What a joyous relief; they hugged and kissed for the first time in two years. They thanked the driver. Bruno slipped him a few bills and said, "Gracie compare."

They were now on there way home. Most of the other relatives were already there. Raffaela was one of the last to arrive. There was as big feast awaiting them. Tired and sick as they were, they ate very little. The women had Raffaela's house as ready as possible. At least they could go to bed for a much needed rest. Their was home made Italian bread freshly baked that day just for them and coffee for their first breakfast in Morrison.

The big black trunk, full of the only possessions they were allowed to bring, was not scheduled to arrive for at least another week. They had traveled the whole trip with only the clothes on their backs. A bath and a clean change of clothing were desperately needed. The aunts and cousins accommodated Raffaela and Frank until the trunk arrived. Bruno promised to buy Raffaela a sewing machine and shop for all her other sewing needs

That weekend, Raffaela and Frank were invited to the boss's house. Mr. Winold's wife and Edith, his daughter, gave gifts as a welcome to all the employees and their families as they arrived. Raffaela and Frank were mortified. She could not speak or understand English. Frank was just as lost. Everyone assured them to not worry. The Winold's were accustomed to this. It would be okay. Raffaela was given a pink glass sugar bowl with matching cream and sugar holders plus a handmade doily that Edith had made. Frank was given a long yellow thing he thought might be fruit, but was not sure. They both graciously said "grazie" and walked back home. Frank had put the banana in his hind pocket. After several hours one of the cousins asked frank why he was doing this. Frank pulled it out of his pocket, looked at it, and asked, "What am I supposed to do with it?" Everyone laughed so hard at this, not meaning to embarrass Frank. Finally, someone took the banana and showed Frank how to peel it and to be brave enough to take a bite. Gingerly, Frank bit off a small morsel. He liked it. Frank's first banana;

CHAPTER 2

The migration of the Serrece

A ll of the families had migrated from the same province of southern Italy to seek employment in the chemical plant located in the village of Morrison. An elderly German, an immigrant himself, supervised it as well as all eight houses. Each one had an outside privy that stood like miniature silhouettes of the houses.

Every house, except one duplex, contained six rooms, living and dining room, three upstairs bedrooms, and a barren kitchen. The brazen big stove and a sink with constant running water were all that signified its use. The oven had gas for baking, but the stovetop had to be fired with coal or wood. At least baking bread was somewhat simplified.

Gaslights kept the house dimly lit. Reading or any other tasks that required good lighting, had to be a daytime task. In the dark cold winter months everyone went to bed shortly after dinner; the potbelly stove in the dining room would be fired for the last time. By midnight, the house would be frigid.

The windows would be coated with a thick layer of ice every morning. Rosie would scrape a circle clean so she could peek out at the snow. Bruno had already been up by five to rekindle the stove so that it would be warm by the time everyone else got up. Bruno's workday began at six in the morning at the plant. Getting used to this drastic change in climate was a very difficult endeavor for every one. They had left a warm mild climate in Italy. This was a hardship for everyone until they became accustomed to it. No one was really very happy with it. They just endured it as best as they could. A day never passed that someone did not speak fondly of their beloved Serra and its sunshine and wonderful fruits and vegetables that were always available

The company paid to have the walls re-papered as everyone moved in. The old paper in Bruno and Raffaela's house was dirty and smoky from the wood and coal stove that was used for heating the house. The previous people were careless about not using wet green wood. Raffaela chose light cheery colors with vines and dainty flowers. Each room was a different color and pattern. Rosie's was a pretty pale pink with wildflowers on it.

The furniture consisted of a dresser that was made from two orange crates put together with a board. A space was left in the middle to allow an ample dresser top to accommodate small items. A ruffled skirt made out of flour sacks concealed its crude identity. There was one in each bedroom plus the bed made for adequate needs. Raffaela's trunk was placed in the dining room. Covered with a flour sack, it served as a buffet top. Bruno made a large wooden table from scrap wood he was given at the sawmill. He spent his evenings carving the wooden legs by hand with a small carving knife. Bruno made two benches for temporary seating. He spent the rest of his spare time that winter making six chairs. The benches now became outside furniture. One was placed on the front porch and the other one was placed at the cool shady side of the house.

This area became the gathering place for the women during the day. In the summer time, each afternoon they would sit for a chat and a cool drink of kool-aide. Each one brought their peas to shell, beans to snap and cut, and potatoes to peel. Raffaela would take her sewing out and work on it as she chatted with everyone. They loved to tell funny stories that happened in thee Serra. This was a time of laughter and memories to be shared.

The women all started their spaghetti sauce early in the morning. As was the customs, the sauce would be left to simmer all day. This came from the fact that fresh tomatoes were used and needed to cook this long in order for the sauce to have a thick succulent flavor to it. The marriage of fresh herbs and tomatoes was an unsurpassed gastronomical treat A pot of beans of assorted varieties, cooked with fennel was a regular accompany to the daily meals. Rosie could hardly wait for dinnertime. She ate very little for breakfast and lunch. She was always too busy with her activities to take time to indulge very much. Dinnertime was Rosie's favorite time of day. She always got a candy treat if she ate all her pasta and vegetables.

Not every ones house was as crude as Rosie's house. Most everyone spent money to make his or her homes comfortable and as attractive as possible. Not Bruno! He sent all his extra funds to a bank in Serra San Bruno, Italy. He had dreams of returning to the villa he and Raffaela had left behind. Bruno's mother and sister Rita were reaping the benefits of everything that they had to leave behind. This was necessary in order that their son would not go hungry and be assured a better life.

Being very aware of the differences in the homes, as young as Rosie was, she was very timid about entering anyone's house for fear she might do something wrong or sit where she was not supposed to sit. Uncle Shorty's house was the exception to this. Rosie was always welcome there any time. Ange and Sue were like her big sisters. Rosie was in awe over the pretty furniture everyone had. The dining room intrigued Rosie most of all. There would be a china cabinet full of pretty dishes for her to admire and dream of having some day. Rosie yearned to sit on one of the soft plush chairs or the big sofa with all the crocheted pillows the women had made. Rosie learned that those rooms were off limits to her and mom and these were for very special company only. Rosie was a little girl who might mess things up. She was always happy to return to her crude house after one of these visits. Raffaela was always offered coffee, but they sat in the kitchen and used old cups.

There was constant running water in the kitchen sink in the wintertime. The pipes would freeze and had to be torched to regain water flow Water was heated in huge tubs for washing dishes, clothes, or for bathing. Bath time was Saturday night for all the female members as well as all the younger people. Showers were provided at the factory for all the men that worked there.

Washing clothes meant several huge tubs of boiling water on a coal-fired stovetop. The more soiled laundry was left to soak until the water-cooled. It was poked around with a big stick to help remove the dirt. Then Frank and Bruno would set the tub on a wooden stand made for that purpose; a washboard was inserted against the side of the tub. A bar of Fels Napa and a lot of scrubbing on the board and the laundry was ready to be rinsed in the large kitchen sink with frigid running water. Each item was rung out by hand and set in a clean tub. In the summertime and nice days, everything was hung out to dry. Bad weather in Rosie's house meant everything was carried up to a spare bedroom that had lines strung across it. After two days the laundry would be ready to take down.

The kitchen table made a sturdy ironing board. Raffaela covered it with an old blanket to protect it from getting burned. The flat iron had to be heated on the stove repeatedly in order to maintain the proper heat.

Life was hard for everyone in this small village. The men worked long hours in the chemical plant for a small pittance. Five dollars was taken off the top for rent each month. They were grateful to have money for food each week. The women tended to the house and gardens and the family.

With the exception of two families, everyone else was related. These families were considered as "compare"; very good friends. Maria had an abundance of great aunts and uncles plus twenty-six second cousins. Frank was ten years older than little Rosie. She adored him from the start. Frank helped with her care and entertainment. Besides the row of houses, there were several homes on the road to Kinzua. They were very friendly, helpful people and we were grateful to them for all their kindnesses.

CHAPTER 3

Serra San Bruno

Although Morrison was nestled below the beautiful hills of Kinzua country, it was no match to the beauty and warmth of southern Italy. It was, to everyone as they arrived a big disappointment.

Morrison had no piaza's with magnificent churches, or great shops containing an assortment of hard to find merchandise. The beautiful fountains, each with a distinct architecture, beckoned people and pigeons to their side. They enjoyed the cool spray of the water each emitted into the air like whales spewing for air as they raced through the ocean.

Serra San Bruno sits on a crest of a mountain just before it declines downward and leads to the sea. Roads that lead into the village are precarious turns of snake and horseshoe

with many ups and downs to complicate traveling even more. There has been a great deal of speculation as to from where these gentle people migrated. One theory is that they are survivors of a volcanic island that had suffered an eruption. They are known as Certosi; they call themselves Serrici. The dialect is so distinct that the first sentences they utter give them completely away. Their cuisine is different from other

regions of Italy. The food has a blend of flavors that indicate more than one nationally. A meal can range from a hot spicy one, to a very mild bland one. Sweets are not a major interest to them. Sponge cakes with fruit topping or variety of biscotti are the popular choices. Wine, fruit and cheese are a must. Surrounding the village, olive orchards dot the hilly countryside. Every year in the fall, they celebrate this beloved gift of food with a huge celebration that lasts for a week.

Many castles and churches are to be found there, but it is the only place that is the home of the Certosi monks. On a hillside way above the town, there is a winding trail that leads to the monastery. It is widely known throughout Italy and many other countries as the Certosi of Serra San Bruno they are the only order known for their silent devotion and solitude. They speak to each other on Sundays; these conversations are related to matter of the church and the village. There time is spent in silent prayer and contemplation. History states that a monk from France by the name of Bruno di Colonia started the order in 1053 AD. Bruno set the very strict rules that are adhered to today.

Bruno's and Raffaela's villa set below the monastery hillside right on the edge of the main village of Serra san Bruno. He was renowned for his good wines he made from his vineyard. Each year, Bruno would share his bounty with the monks. He would fill a large basket with the best grapes. Then he and Frank would tract up the windy patch that lay near the side of the property to pay the monks a solemn visit. The monks acknowledged the generous gift with nods and gestures. Bruno would wish them well, make the sign of the cross, bow, and down the path homeward. As they walked down the path, Bruno could not help but think about the monk's bazaar method of burying their dead. They were thrown in a mass grave. This seemed very disrespectful of their monks who had served their lives in honor of God and man.

Most Calabresi are short and stocky people. There are a few tall thin people as well; possibly a result of many different nationalities. Prominent hair and eye colors are brown and black, but it is not unusual to see blonde or red hair and green or blue eyes.

Calabresi are always ready to give a helping hand when and wherever it is needed. They will drop everything that they are doing to lend a hand. Weddings are a big important event. All buttons are pulled for these great events. There is more than enough help available if needed. Dancing continuous into the next morning. Their classic tarantella never seems to tire them.

It is no wonder then, that those that chose to leave to a better world or were forced to do so after World War 1 never lost sight of who they were. The same rules applied to those that chose Morrison, PA. Many friends and relatives live in nearby communities. No one ever needs to be alone or in need of a helping hand.

CHAPTER 4

Malo Ochio

The paganism attitude that truly irritated Rosie and several younger people was the "Mal Occhio" or The Bad Eye. They believed that if a person that was not totally in their favor for any reason and they gave you an evil eye, you would fall ill to their wishes. Sister in laws are a good example of this situation. Jealousy and different opinions lead to dissidence between them and their families.

One particular male relative believed so strongly on the "Mal Occhio" that he accused his brother's wife of this terrible deed. The two women were not compatible but the accused one really was a gentle person that minded to her own affairs.

She supposedly gave the "Mal Occhio" to her sister in law, thus succumbing her to permanent illness. If this had been kept just between them, it would have been controllable. However, this male relative, who was otherwise well respected, made it difficult for everyone. Nothing anyone would say to him could convince him otherwise. In order to keep the peace, it was a silent understanding that we had to pretend not to associate ourselves with anyone of "Zia's" household when "Zio" was in view. This made it hellacious for all of "Zia's" family and us. My father with his oil ceremony did not ever stand for this and did as he chose to. Because of his high respect, "Zio" did not dare challenge him.

In the meantime, "Zio's" wife became steadily worse. We tried to get him to take her for medical help, but he truly believed "Zia" would have to lift the curse or his wife would not get better. What isolation and the lack of education, this is what superstition does to humans. After several years of suffering, the oldest daughter took her to a doctor who diagnosed her as having terminal cancer. It had spread over 80 percent of her body. I watched lay in her bed dying for six months. At death she weighed 85 pounds. What a waste. Still "Zio" stubbornly never changed his attitude. "Zio" finally moved to Warren when he found a job there. Eventually I got to know my cousins better without any guilt attached.

Catholicism ran hand in hand with paganism. The oil ceremony is a good example of this. Should anyone in Morrison become ill, Bruno was called upon to perform the oil ceremony on him or her. Bruno had been bestowed the sacred rights of a healer as a young man. Out would come a special basin, warm water was poured into this as Bruno said a prayer. Then olive oil would be poured into a small chalice like cup. Bruno would start chanting a special prayer and make the sign of the cross. Then as he continued with more prayers he would dip his two for fingers into the oil, sprinkles the oil into the basin, and this was repeated several times. Then Bruno would count the large spread drops. If they were more than the smaller ones, it meant the person was very ill. As Bruno re-anointed the persons forehead he would recite the final prayer of healing. If they did not get better in a day or two, Dr. Flat would be summoned immediately. Bruno had to bestow these sacred powers on one of his children. He hoped Rosie would accept this high honor.

Rosie had been a very bright active child; except for one thing. She refused to walk by herself since her mishap. She had fallen and gotten badly bruised by getting splinters in her hand.

Bruno was tired of carrying Rosie all over; she was a heavy rolly polly girl and needed to walk on her own. One day Bruno carried Rosie out to the garden and set her down in the pea patch. He handed Rosie a handful of peas, then started to harvest the rest of the peas into a basket. Rosie ate all the peas, and then she spotted a very large one high on a pole. Very carefully Rosie got up and took a shaky unsure first step. Then she let go of the pole and walked over to that prize pea pod Rosie wanted so badly. Bruno's trick had worked. Rosie was walking (on her own) at last. Taking Rosie's hand, he then walked her up and down the road in front of the houses as Rosie chanted "Comino, Comino", "I'm walking! I'm walking!" Everyone came out onto the porches clapping and cheering Rosie. This made Rosie very proud of herself. Bruno was to wonder if he regretted his getting Rosie to walk after all as there was no stopping her now. She kept everyone tired chasing after her.

Since Rosie's world consisted of her father mother, brother and the rest of the community that surrounded her, Rosie was a happy child. She looked forward to any events that took place in Morrison. In the summertime everyone would gather around a big bob fire for an evening of song and dance. Frank would play his mouth organ and guitar at the same time Rosie had to hold the mouth organ for him since he did not have a holder for it. He also played the mandolin in between songs. "Compare" Rocco played a Spanish guitar, chanting 'brm bem brm' as he strummed the strings. Toots played the accordion and the squeeza boxa. Everyone sang songs of the Serra that they all remembered from their beloved homeland and the U.S. born cousins sang country western tunes that were popular at the time. Rosie loved to sing two of her favorite songs; You Are My Sunshine and O Solo mio, then everyone would start clapping and chanting "balla balla".

Rosie knew it was her turn to dance the Tarantella. Needless to say Rosie was more than happy to entertain everyone.

Springtime 1940, Rosie was anxiously waiting to be accepted into first grade. She had been vaccinated as was required but sadly she was told she missed the deadline by two weeks and would have to wait another year. She had sat on the front porch bench for the last two years watching everyone come and go up the road to the little white schoolhouse that was at the end of the big field. Since there was no one to play with or go for walks with, Rosie passed her time away with the old folks. Quick to catching on to everything, she soon learned to sew aprons and doll clothes. Raffaela was not in good health at the time. So Rosie helped with the household chores her favorite job was to pull down all the dark green shades in the afternoon. Then they would open all the doors and school all the flies out the door by waving and batting a big towel at them. Since there were no screens anywhere, they would come back in. as soon as the doors were opened again. Sticky tap hung in every room, but these filled up quickly. At least some reprieve was given during the evening meal.

Meals to Rosie meant pasta, beans, and rice in any combination with or without tomato sauce. Early May everyone would take bushel baskets and go dandelion digging. Wild mushrooms came later. The greens would be cleaned of bad leaves and the root cut off. After several washings, they were ready to be boiled until tender. There was always a pot of beans cooked and ready for many uses. The women would fry onion greens, ad the beans and dandelions until they were sot and all the extra liquid was evaporated then a little tomato sauce left over from the previous nights meal, would be added along with a few more spices and grating cheese. These was simmered till the sauce was absorbed and thickened for five weeks or until the dandelions flowered this was the staple meal of the day.

Mushrooming began as soon as the weather warmed and the rains came regularly. Rosie would go get a basket so she could go with Raffaela to find her favorite pink mushrooms; every one learned quickly which ones were safe to eat.

Every March, Bruno would bring the dirt boxes down from the attic. These were to be used for starting the seedlings for the coming garden. Rosie was allowed to help plant the tiny seeds that had been dried and saved from last years garden. A pencil hole was made an in inch apart throughout the whole box; then one seed was dropped into each one. These were then covered lightly with sifted soil and watered. It was now time for Rosie to watch the magic of the seeds turn into little plants and grow up to produce such yummy vegetables such as tomatoes, peppers, cucumbers and broccoli. The rest of the veggies were planted from seed directly into the soil in the best location for them. Every one planted the same vegetables. The gardens were carbon copies of each other, but Bruno had a greener thumb than the others. He always had bigger tomatoes and peppers than anyone else plus bigger crops of everything else. All the gardens thrived very well each summer. We ate what was necessary to sustain us for the summer. Of any veggies that could be preserved, the rest was either canned or cured in salt brine set in crocks with a wooden lid held down with a large stone.

Every June, "Zia" Assunta, Toots mother, would come to get Rosie to go strawberry picking along the road to Kane. She would make a pouch of her large apron and tie it to her dress belt. Rosie would grab her biggest Easter basket that now was very empty. Hand in hand they would walk past the little white schoolhouse. The berries grew in profusion from the spring that was a few hundred feet from the school all the way to the house that had burnt down. By the time they picked both sides of the road the apron would be overflowing with berries and Rosie's basket was mounded as high as the handle. Rosie had to be careful or she could lose a lot of big berries as they walked back home. "Zia" Assunta never kept any berries for herself. She knew how much Rosie loved them and always gave them all to her. Raffaela canned a few pints and made some jam to enjoy during the winter months. The rest Rosie shared for a dessert treat with sugar and canned milk. Rosie always took a jar of jam to "Zia" after each picking for them to enjoy on fresh baked bread.

The men went blackberry and thimbleberry picking. A risky adventure at that, everyone carried a sharp hoe and pushed the bushes carefully aside before ever getting near them. Many a rattler met its death at the end of a hoe. Berries were very abundant on the sunny hillsides around the village. Everyone came home with two large pails a day for over two weeks. Fresh berry Italian pies called flans were baked daily. The rest were canned or turned into luscious jam with honey made our jam special. Bruno would go honeycombing and he would drain them for the best sweetener Mother Nature could provide for us, free! In the fall, everyone joined in apple picking in the surrounding deserted orchards. Was Johnny Apple Seed perhaps responsible for all the trees? John Chapman was known to have spent time in this area. Applesauce would waif from one end of the houses to the other. The northern spies and green rustys' were saved to enjoy eating through out the cold winter months. These were stored in the basement in large sacks that were insured into wooden barrels. Next came the nut harvest, butternut, black walnuts and hazelnut trees were scattered here and there amongst the wooded areas. They took the most time to gather since a larger area had to be covered to acquire enough of them. The nuts would be spread out on burlap bags to dry for several months. Then we would bring down a few at a time to hull. The coating on the hulls would turn our hands brown for weeks.

In the winter evenings, the women would sew or knit while the men gathered for an Italian card game called Briscola. A big bowl of assorted nuts set in the center of the table with a hammer on top. All night the ping of the hammer would keep Rosie awake. She then would tiptoe into the room with her hands cupped; "walla" it was filled with shelled nuts for her. How did they know she was coming?

Rosie was becoming very aware of her surroundings and all the changes that came with each season. Summers that were long hot, steamy days were waning into shorter, cooler fall days. The emeralds of the hillsides were beginning to turn into hues of ruby and gold; Mother Nature was kept very busy with her autumn paintbrush. She had very limited time in which she could accomplish her special task; old man winter was hovering nearby to take his turn.

As the leaves began to fall, Rosie was in awe over the beautiful carpet they provided as a finale to the season. Rosie loved to go shuffling her feet through the leaves on the long walks she took with anyone that would take her.

Frank made Rosie a slingshot and taught her how to shoot it. Then he took her hunting for squirrels and chipmunks. It was very hard for Rosie to kill these cute animals, but she resolved to either food for their table or dinner for the foxes. Frank convinced Rosie it was not any different than fishing and Rosie loved to go fishing with Frank! After all the squirrels did make a tasty treat in spaghetti sauce.

CHAPTER 5

"Natale"

Very soon Christmas, "Natale", would be upon us. Frank and all the other older boys would head to the hillside in deep snow carrying an axe and a long rope. Only seven trees were to be chopped down for Christmas. Only the larger trees passed the test to become this seasons 'precept' Christmas tree. Frank always picked a bushel of soft green moss before the snow came to cover it. He put it in the basement to keep it moist then frank would make a hillside scene under the tree that had been put on a platform. The moss would then transform this into a magical setting for the manger. Frank carefully set each ceramic image of the people and animals that were there to give adoration to the newborn king, Jesus. Rosie helped to then arrange and hang the glass bulbs and tinsel. Since electricity was a wonder and not a Morrison commodity, there were not any lights used on the tree. A large red candle set on a nearby stand illuminated the magic of the "precipo". Christmas time was the most exciting and important time of the year for all of Morrison. The men hunted for deer and turkey; some would come home with several rabbits as well. Everyone shared his or her bounty with everyone else. No one was to be left out of a good feast. Since it was always very cold the month of December, venison hanging on the side porches of each house was a common sight. Hopefully some could be saved for steak cutlets for Christmas day. Ground venison was transformed into luscious meatballs the whole month of December. All the women and older girls were busy baking a variety of yummy biscotti, specialty breads, and torta sicka (which is a very hard candy that had to be broken into small pieces with a hammer.) All the older men already had made their prized "Vino" during grape harvest time. Each boasted that their wine would be the best tasting. This assured them the excuse to partake of several glasses of wine at everyone's house to affirm their vote. Bruno usually won. He never lost his touch from his homeland. Rosie always looked foreword to squashing the grapes and turning her hands purple.

Every family raised at least one pig that would provide them with all the winter cured meats. November was hog slaughtering time. Rosie hated this. Her pig that she fondly had helped to feed all summer was to be killed. Rosie would run up to her bedroom in tears and cover her head with two pillows. The sound of the pigs squalling terrified her. This went on until all the hogs had been butchered. Since this animals weighed up to six hundred pounds each, it took at least four men to handle them. Therefore each hog was scheduled to be slaughtered several days apart. This usually went on for two weeks. Poor Rosie would be a basket case by the time this process ended.

After the meat hung for a couple of days. It was brought in one section at a time and cut into whatever use was decided for it. The prize meat on the chops became Cappocola and the hindquarters became hams. The rest was ground and to be made into sausages. Some were left fresh and the rest were cured. Sopra satta and pepperoni was also made. The casings had to be rid of the fetus. Then after several washings they were soaked in cold salt and vinegar water overnight. These had to be rinsed again several times before they were ready to use. The Cappacola was the easiest. It was smothered in hot ground pepper after it had soaked in salt brine for a day. They were inserted into the largest casing. A hanger was fashioned from a regular coat hanger it was now ready to go to the makeshift spare room that was turned into a smokehouse. The ground meat was seasoned specially for its designated purpose and put into the smaller casing. All were hung in the smoke house. A large pail full of charcoal was kept burning at a low temperature at all time. A window was always open to allow ventilation during the whole process.

Mist of the smaller sausages would be ready by Christmastime. Bruno had sunk a portion of the meat into the Kinzua creek along side the pigpens. This was put into a sealed barrel that had a rope tied around it. He secured the rope to a small tree at the side of the creek. This assured us that we would have fresh meat for several weeks past Christmas. Raffaela made meatballs and tasty cutlets out of the best parts. Some was just cooked in the sauce in large chunks or fresh sausages were made. Bruno had a black and white cow that he grazed on the other side of the tracks below the pigpens in the winter she was housed in a small shelter he had made for her. She was milked daily and gave us more than we could use. Raffaela would fill a large kettle with the fresh warm milk. This would be gentled simmered till she was sure it was safe to drink. Ricotta was made daily and what was left Bruno made into basket cheese and grating cheese. There was always an ample supply of mozzarella and provolone available and Bruno shared very generously with everyone,

Christmas eve was a night of dining with the families; the menu consisted of pesce stucco [dried cod] and polenta with cheese and sauce and pasta with oil and garlic. The relish tray was laden with home cured green olives, green tomatoes, peppers; hot and sweet, eggplant and pickled beets. Piti were made earlier in the day. This is a soft doughnut like bread dough, sticky as all get out, which was formed into large balls with pepperoni, anchovy, or a chunk of cheese in the center. We were only permitted to partake of the meatless ones that evening, since no meat was permitted on Christmas Eve.

Bruno had saved all year in order to be able to buy the entire holiday goodies foe the family. Figs, chestnuts, cactus pears, oranges, and Bosc pears were overflowing in a large basket thanks to his thoughtfulness. Rosie loved the cactus pears the best. Bruno would put on his heavy leather gloves then carefully pick up the biggest pear, cut off both ends, slice it open and let Rosie pluck the luscious sweet treat that this melon colored fruit encased in a green prickly thick skin. Santa Claus always came early on Christmas morning. He didn't have a chimney to slide down and get all dirty and he didn't bring his reindeer, but he always had a big red sack slung over his shoulders. 'He' would enter in the back door without knocking and chirp ho' ho' ho'; Buon Natale! Rosie would run and hide under the precipo. It was not because she was afraid, but she knew that Sanyo Colosimo was really Lucy Defabio playing Santa Claus. Something was wrong that was for sure. All Rosie got was an orange to add to the overflowing basket of fruit on the table end. S much for Santa Claus is coming to town; he probably got lost and could not find Morrison on any map.

After Lucy left, Rosie got out the Christmas outfit that Raffaela had spent months making for her. It was a soft dark red velvet dress with pearl buttons and a white Satan sash sporting a big bow. Raffaela also made Rosie a matching red coat and bonnet to keep Rosie warm. Frank gave her a pair of mittens and a new pair of black Patton leather shoes. Rosie found a new pair of stockings under the tree. All this made Rosie very happy; she didn't care if Santa ever came! Her family did not forget her.

Everyone in Morrison went to church in Kane for Christmas mass and it was round trip caravan. Then the afternoons were spent taking a token gift to everyone. It was more like musical chairs since everybody was doing the same thing. Then it would be time to finish preparing the Christmas feast. Pasta and meatballs, venison steaks, sausages, and sometimes rabbit or chicken filled a large serving dish. Pasta was served first and separate from the meat dishes and usually after a warm bowl of chicken soup. Then came the relish dish and last the meat and salad. A glass of wine was always full during this feast. Coffee and biscotti were served last after the cheese and fruit. Rosie would be stuffed, but never to full to enjoy a toroni; a soft creamy, Nugent confection that was coated with a crisp wafer. This Rosie washed down with a glass of homemade eggnog laced with a little bit of wine. It did not take Rosie long to roll into bed and fall fast asleep. Buon Natale until next year!

New year's day signaled a new beginning; a time of hope and aspirations. Everyone had been thinking about the new years resolutions they would make. They never lasted very long, but at least some effort was made. Storytelling at least was dependable. John Tassone was our fable king. He knew every story from the Serra that anyone could imagine. The guys played their favorite 'band' songs and several Italian songs. Then we would indulge in the last of the biscotti and more of broncos eggnog. Beer and wine were always available for the guys. This gathering was held at our house or Uncle Shorty's with a cheery buon Serra we would all go home and hope for an early spring to save us.

Rosiest big birthday party

By Valentines Day, the snow started to melt and the Kinzua creek started to overflow. Gratefully it turned cold again, so the threat of flooding was over for the time being, since everyone was accustomed to this happening every year; quickly forgotten by all except Raffaela. She still panicked for she had a great fear of water.

Old man winter finally gave in to the warmth of the springtime sunshine around Rosie's birthday. She had been anxiously waiting her sixth birthday. Bruno had promised Rosie a party with a big birthday cake. Bruno baked a huge three-tier cake; he had made the tins out of oilcans. Then he got the brainstorm to make egg white frosting. Four people took turns beating six egg whites that had been set outside to stay cool. The hot sugar mixer did not faze them. (The only mixer we had is two forks held together.) After an hour of this procedure, Toots talked Bruno into giving up. He had to resort to a regular confectioner sugar butter cream frosting. Rosie was pleased with it. Everyone in Morrison was invited for cake and coffee. Rosie's penny jar was filled to the top. That was the best celebration ever'

Joyously, Easter arrived the end of March. Rosie loved to go to church on Palm Sunday for the blessed palms everyone received. These Rosie fashioned into various size crosses for her family and one for Asunta. Then Rosie anxiously awaited the arrival of "Compare" Mike; her godfather. He always brought Rosie a huge Easter basket filled with jellybeans, chocolate eggs and money. A big chocolate bunny stood on his hind legs peering at Rosie to tempt her. The whole basket was covered with noisy yellow paper. There was no way Rosie could cheat and get into it before dinner. This was an annoying hardship for Rosie since she very rarely got candy the rest of the year. Rosie was getting tired of pasta no matter how it was embellished. She had seen American food at the Winold's house several times and yearned to have some of it. Right now all Rosie wanted was her Easter basket and hoped Raffaela would have the pasta cooked very soon.

Bruno promised Rosie that he would take her to the bank with him on his next visit since Rosie had not been photographed since she was two years old. They decided to have that done at the same time as the bank trip. Dressed up like a little princess, with a big white bow in her hair, Rosie proudly walked in the door of Warren National Bank. The whole bank personal fell in love with this adorable friendly little girl. Rosie and Bruno were escorted by one of the tellers to the enclosed area that the vaults were kept. Bruno tuned the round knob to several numbers until he heard a click then he turned the big handle and the huge door opened to reveal all of Bruno's belongings. Rosie was so impressed that she let out a little squeal of delight. Bruno showed Rosie a ring that he said would some day belong to Rosie. Rosie tried it on it was such a beautiful red stone with a shiny gold band. But of course it was much too large for Rosie just yet. As Bruno and Rosie started to leave the bank, Rosie waved saying "grazie bebbe donne" [thank you nice ladies], but not before Rosie was presented a metal bank that was a replica of the original bank. Rosie could not believe it. There was money in it and a little key was taped to the roof so that Rosie could take her money out whenever she chose to. This proved to be too often, so Bruno hid the key on Rosie. This did not deter Rosie from getting out her precious loot when she wanted to buy candy on their shopping trips. She took one of Raffaela's hairpins and passed up the opening to spread the teeth apart. Success! The whole lout fell onto Rosie's lap. She always left a penny in there. Frank still kept giving Rosie all his change for her to put into the bank. He thought it was funny that Rosie figured out how to get her change without a key. Bruno wasn't very impressed at all.

The rest of that spring and summer was spent getting Rosie s wardrobe ready for school. This was done on free time between all the chores that normally had to be done such as gardening and canning. Raffaela made Rosie three dresses out of flour sacks she had been saving, a white petticoat out of a sheet that had ripped in the middle and a warm jacket from new material. Rosie helped by removing the stitches sewing the buttons on and keeping a needle threaded at all times for Raffaela.

CHAPTER 6

Grocery shopping

Although there were home deliveries to Morrison, for food and other needs, Bruno preferred to shop for his own groceries. For those without transportation, home delivery service was a blessing. However many of these shady entrepreneurs had to be bartered with. They attempted to gain a very high profit by inflating the prices of certain very needed items. This they tried to pacify with a cheap token gift. Since there were no fools in Morrison, these shysters got bargained down to size. Either he does it our way or no more orders for them. Kinzua was not a far walk and Bruno was always willing to help out. They would manage. Guess who won out.

A few homes had ice-boxes [ica boxa]. These were a short stocky version of the nice white electric refrigerator unlike what "Zia" Cenca had. It was completely made of wood with a big metal tray sunk into the bottom shelf. This slid in and out to make replacing the ice block convenient every Friday morning before the groceries arrived. The ice truck would come and replace the melted icy water with a fresh huge block of ice. The rest of the families including Bruno kept the perishables in the small cellar under the kitchen. They were made of heavy stonewalls, dirt floors and a thick wooden door that had tar paper on both sides of it. This was concealed with a metal trap door.

Little Rosie loved to go shopping. She was always assured a five-cent strawberry ice cream cone and a package of her favorite biscotti. Bruno alternated between shopping in Kane and in Warren. This way they could acquire in one place that the other did not carry.

What worried Rosie was getting there and back home. The 'T' had a leaky roof. Bruno attempted several times to tar it, but it never held. Knowing very well the rain would drip onto the seat next to Rosie, this gave Rosie the task of overseeing the pans position so that all the rain dripped into the pan without tipping over. As if that was not bad enough, the radiator always boiled over. It needed a new thermostat and Bruno kept putting off replacing it. Bruno would pull over to the side of the road, open the hood to let the steam out and head for the nearest stream or spring. He would return with his white straw hat full of water; the pan was much too small and shallow for this task. Rosie and Raffaela knew it would happen again on the way home. We were grateful that Kinzua country was blessed with several small streams and springs that came tumbling down the hillsides

The main attraction on the way home from Kane was stopping to see the lobo wolves. The owner of the log cabin and restaurant called Limberlost had them penned off the back of the restaurant. Bruno explained to Rosie that they were being hunted too much and soon there would not be any more wolves. This kind man was trying to save them from this peril. They had an eerie howl that terrified Raffaela. Wolves initially were harmful to humans and looked upon as a bad omen. Rosie liked to hear the echo of their howls on the surrounding hills. They looked like big dogs to her.

Besides shopping, the trip to Warren always included visiting friends and relatives. "Zia" Cenca had moved to warren when Rosie was still a baby. Rosie loved "Zia" and all her big cousins, which were always there. Jean was like a big sister to Rosie. Babe spoiled her with all the attention that she loved. "Zia" always gave Rosie a pretty piece of jewelry and a bag of candy.

Food immediately appeared from out of nowhere. Zia always had salami, cheese, fried peppers, and potatoes on hand. Also mountains of sliced freshly baked bread. Oh yes; don't forget Rosie's favorite black olives. Wine and beer were offered generously since the restaurant and bar was well supplied with them. Rosie loved Coca Cola and washed her food down with a big bottle of it.

Rosie wished they would move to Warren. Everybody had such nice houses with pretty furniture. Best of all there was a room called the bathroom upstairs in "Zia's" house. It had a big shiny white tub that one could sit in without curling all up, a shiny faucet turned on to magically poor hot and cold water into the tub for a luxurious bath, a sink that had faucets that turned on and off, and a commode with a shiny pink seat. There were no Sears or Montgomery ward catalogs to be used for tissue paper. On the wall was a roller that held soft white paper that Rosie could tear off to use. Fascinated by it all, Rosie gingerly pushed down the handle like big cousin Jean had showed her, watching the miracle of a flushing toilet. Then she carefully turned on the faucet to wash her hands. The warm water felt good as it trickled between Rosie's fingers and then disappeared down the drain. Rosie carefully dried her hands on the pretty flowered towel and hung it back careful to not wrinkle it. Rosie then tiptoed back down the long stairway. She heard new voices that she recognized. Her godmother Rose, "Zia's" oldest daughter and younger sister Ange had just come in the door. "Comari" Rose always greeted Rosie with a warm smile and asked, "How's Morrison? Rosie would answer, "Still there; it won't go away". This brought a laugh or two out of everyone.

They said their goodbyes and thank-yous with a promise to return again very soon. On the way home, Rosie listened to her father explain to her mother that they too would have to decide where to move to. There were rumors of a big reservoir called a dam that was going to be built soon. Bruno pointed to the Allegheny River where he thought it would start. That meant Kinzua and Morrison, plus all the surrounding areas, would be under water. Raffaela and Rosie hoped the move would come soon and that it would be Warren.

PART 2

CHAPTER 1

Rosie goes to school

The first day of school finally arrived. Rosie was so excited that she has gotten ready an hour early and tried to get Frank to hurry. She would finally be able to learn to read and write in English. Rosie already wrote in Italian very well. Bruno had started teaching her when she was two years old. Rosie had a cousin that she wrote to in Sydney, Australia. Since Louie could not read Italian, Uncle Sam had to read the letters to him. Rosie could not wait to surprise Louie with a letter written in English. Rosie knew that she was good in math, so that did not bother her for now.

Rosie proudly walked up the road to the little white schoolhouse, holding onto to Frank's hand. This would be Frank's last year of school for him. He would not be taking the bus to the big school in Kinzua like some of the other cousins did. Frank would be working with Bruno cutting wood. We were poor so Frank had to do his share.

Frank walked Rosie in the door, found her seat for her, and then walked over to his usual seat. All eight grades were in one room and 80 percent of the students were Rosie and Frank's cousins. Stella, one of the cousins happened to be seated in front of Rosie. This was Stella's second year so Rosie figured that she knew everything about reading and writing. Miss Printice handed Rosie her very first reading book. Rosie quickly opened it to the first page to see a boy running. She guessed at the words but could not read them. Tapping Stella on her shoulder, she asked if she would help her read the words. Stella read 'run Dick, run. Jane can run'.

Rosie had heard that Miss Printice was a suspicious mean lady that loved to break orange crate boards on anyone's backside if prompted. These were supposed to be used to fire the potbelly stove that sat in the front of the room. Rosie was being accused of slandering Miss Printice in Italian. If at anytime anyone wanted to say something that was not any business of Miss Printice, they would converse in Italian. She always took this

suspiciously and personally,.

Miss Printice grabbed Rosie by the nap of her neck and pulled her to the front of the room saying, "I'll teach you a lesson little whop girl that you will not ever forget". She started hitting Rosie on her backside with a stick she had picked up near the stove. It hurt, but Rosie held back the tears. She wanted to go back to her book. Miss Printice was infuriated because Rosie would not cry, so she picked up another stick and was about to hit Rosie with it when all of a sudden all the big boys got up, formed a chain line, and headed toward Miss Printice. She dropped the stick and ran to her car. Frank picked Rosie up and consoled her. The rest blocked the car so that Miss Printice could not try to leave. Toots threatened to let all the air out of the tires if she started the engine. Jeff firmly stated he would bare a whole orange crate on her legs if she ever tried hitting anyone again. No one better ever hurt Rosie if they knew what was good for them. Miss Printice never hit anyone again. Although Miss Printice frowned on anyone taking his or her books home, Rosie managed to get away with it. She made sure she always had it with her the next day. Frank became her new teacher and soon she was reading her third book and doing work assignments in it. These amazed Miss Printice but she never complimented or encouraged Rosie in any way. Rosie did not care, she was happy with what she was doing and proud of her accomplishments. Now she could write to Louie in English all the time.

CHAPTER 2

The mad deer

The last day of school was a very hot, humid 85 degrees. It had been raining during the night leaving a haze all around the surrounding hills.

Miss Printice has left the side door open for air. It was level to the ground and lead to the privies. The front door was open as well. Six steps had to be dealt with into the room. These were shaky wooden planks and a rickety railing

Most of the morning had been spent to clean the room. Everything was to be packed into boxes for the summer. There was a rumor that this was going to be the last year for the little white schoolhouse.

It was almost lunchtime. Everyone usually ran home, gulped down lunch and ran back. Rosie heard someone say, "Oh no". A buck had just bounded into the room from the side door. Normally this was not a problem. It was easy to get the deer back out with a treat. This happened at least twice a year. Not this one. It was frothing at the mouth, snorting, bucking, and kicking all the desks and chairs over. We all ran out the front door. The guys just jumped off the steps. Frank slammed the door shut and picked Rosie up to. Jeff ran home and came back with his rifle. But by the time he got there, the raging creature was running back up the hill out of sight. Jeff wanted to go after it but the other guys talked him out of it. All this time, Miss Printice was hiding in her car.

Apprehensively, we all walked back into the room. What a mess! Everyone's hard work was history. Chairs were tipped over, some broken beyond repair; desks were pushed together and on their sides. There were books and paper everywhere. We all pitched in and put the room back in an orderly fashion as much as was possible. Forget our taking anything home. The guys burned all the damaged furniture fueled by all the books and paper. It was the biggest bond fire Morrison had ever had. Our families were all watching, perplexed and curious.

By the time we finished, we had all missed our lunch. For once in her life, Miss Prentice showed a little compassion. She thanked us. Can you believe it? Thanked us for all the help we had given her. "You are all dismissed. Have a nice summer. I will mail all of you your report card." It was hard to believe these words came out of her mouth.

It did not take us long to go running down the road towards home. We watched her as she drove away toward Ludlow. "Ciao Bella meastra ce bene a la casa." (Goodbye, you're a nice teacher when you go home.) We never saw her again.

On our way home, we saw Duffy our village hermit,. He lived in a run down hut by Sugar Run and walked everywhere. He was a friendly sole, but we all kept our distance. Bathing was not in his dictionary. Once a rattler bit him. He spit out some chewing tobacco, slapped it on the bite, and kept walking. Duffy sported a bushy beard, chewing tobacco encrusted on it, at all times. He carried a poke tied to the end of a stick that he slung over his shoulder. We thought perhaps he put his catch of the day in it. That meant anything he found to be edible. Since he never carried a gun, we assumed he used a slingshot and a fishing fork for his days catch. He probably snared any larger game close to his hut.

The week after school was out, Rosie was sitting on the front porch embroidering a scarf for her orange dresser. Lunchtime was a short time away. The smell of sauce and beans permeated the air from one end of the houses to the other. Rosie was getting hungry, then she heard a strange noise. Looking up from her scarf, she could not believe her eyes, Across from Rosie's house along the oil well, a huge black bear was up on his hunches sniffing and snorting. Rosie froze for a moment, then dropped her scarf and ran into the house shutting the door and all the windows. Raffaela was mortified and did not know what to do. Then Rosie remembered that Bruno had told her bears ran when they heard gunshot. Rosie ran and got two large pans and started clanging them together to sound like a gun. It worked. The bear got down on all four feet and lumbered up the field behind the schoolhouse. Since we lived there by any large game, this became the evening's conversation piece. Others had seen it also and just ran into their houses. The guys thought that the smell of all the food drove him down nears the houses. Was the smell of spaghetti sauce driving him insane? If he ever came back, Bruno was the one anxious to shoot it. What would they do with a 600 lb bear? As long as it never came closer to the houses, they decided let it go. Rosie called it the Italian bear. We never saw it again. Someone may have shot it.

CHAPTER 3

Job hunting

Bruno feared that his job at the Morrison plant would soon come to an end. Woodcutting meant a lot of driving to the locations that were being harvested at present. Therefore job hunting was eminent as soon as possible.

Bruno and Frank left early every morning to look for employment. Finally, by the end of the week, Bruno announced that he and Frank would be working at the chemical plant in Westline part time and cutting wood the rest of the time.

It took two days to get everything ready to go. Two washtubs held everything in the kitchen. It consisted of the canned goods and dry goods such as flour sugar and pasta. Raffaela's precious china was wrapped in towels before placing it carefully into a large canning kettle.

Bruno's "compare" arrived with his model 'T' Ford truck. It had a long bed and sideboards to prevent things from falling out. The men loaded the truck until no more would fit anywhere. a few things stayed behind for the following day when Bruno returned to get the pig. The chickens were loaded first. They were in a small pen Bruno quickly made for this purpose. The cow was sold back to Mr. Offi. There was no place to graze her in Westline.

Rosie had bittersweet feelings about leaving, but she vowed to never return to that little white school in Morrison. Raffaela was saddened, and did not want to leave. She had not been very happy about coming to America. Leaving all her family and friends in her beloved Serra and coming to the woods of Morrison was humiliating enough, but at least she was among relatives and friends. Now she was going to be confined to days of isolation and loneliness in a place where she new no one.

Frank rode in the truck with compare. Bruno, Raffaela, and Rosie led the way to the new house in Westline. The trip was only about twenty miles away, but it may as well have been a hundred. With each mile a deeper void insured in Raffaela.

The house was a larger version of the company houses in Morrison. It had one grand room with a step-up kitchen and three bedrooms. In a short time the truck was unloaded. Everything was carried to the big room. Raffaela had made a large pot of chicken soup the previous day for their evening meal in the new house. "Compare" enjoyed a large bowl of soup and a glass of wine before he left to go back home. Bruno thanked him with a gift of mozzarella cheese and a bottle of Chianti wine. Since the beds had been made immediately upon arrival every one retired early.

The next morning, Rosie got several itchy sores. Rosie asked Raffaela to look at her sores that were all over her arms and legs. Raffaela thought they were mosquito bites since the door had been left open late. She then anointed Rosie's sores with salve to relieve the itching. The next two mornings were a repeat of the first one. Frank went into Rosie's bedroom. He lifted up the covers of the bed expecting to find spiders. The mattress was covered with bed bugs. He pulled all the covers off and took them out to the porch. Then he carefully carried the mattress with the sheets still on it to the back yard. Raffaela had a few bites as well as Bruno. Frank checked their mattress. Bed bugs; Frank had a few on his mattress. He decided to take all the bedding and mattresses outside. Then he took the bed frames out to be sprayed with a pesticide. The mattresses had to be burned. It was the only way to get rid of the bugs. All the bedding was washed with hot soapy bleach water, rinsed several times and hung out to dry.

Fortunately, nothing had been unpacked. There was no way the family could live here with bed bugs and cockroaches. Bruno talked to the owner of the small house he had passed up for this one. Since it was still available, the Raffaele could move in anytime. The factory supervisor offered Bruno the hand trolley to move everything. Rosie thought was fun, but it was hard work for Bruno and Frank. Raffaela would not ride on the trolley, so Bruno drove her down to the little house in the 'T'. He then walked back to other house to help Frank finish loading the trolley with their meager possessions,

Everything was left on the deck and carefully checked over before it was brought into the house. Since there was not enough time to clean the house thoroughly only the bedrooms were scrutinized. Before the bed frames were put into place, since the mattresses were burned, several blankets were laid on the frame for sleeping on that night. That was not very comfortable to say the least. They all had backaches the next morning. Bruno and Frank gulped down bread and coffee, then they were off to Kane to look for mattresses. The owner of the second hand store Bruno knew had just what they needed. He assured Bruno that the mattresses had come from a good clean family that had moved out of state.

It took two trips to transport the mattresses to westline on the 'T's' roof. That night everyone had a comfortable good nights sleep. The next chore was to return to the bughouse and retrieve the pig. Squealing and snorting they pushed him onto the trolley and tied him to the handle. Down the tracks they went very slowly so the pig would not panic too much. The chickens were still in the pen so they were not a problem. Frank put a rope around the pigs' neck that was long enough to take him to the large penned area that once was a dog pen. The chickens were set on the back deck for the time being.

After getting settled, Rosie met a three-year-old girl named Shirley that lived next door. Rosie was glad to have someone to play with. Frank hung the swing up for them to share. Shirley's mother suggested that perhaps Rosie could go to Sunday school at the little white church past the train station. Shirley was already attending classes and was delighted to have Rosie go with her for the rest

of the season. Rosie enjoyed the church very much. She had lots of fun doing art projects and reading from the bible in English. Rosie met several nice girls there as well. But Rosie wondered where the boys were and why didn't they come to bible school? Rosie was soon to find out.

Westline sets in the midst of what is known as black cherry country. It is a coveted wood used for many things, especially furniture, and is in great demand. What upset Bruno was the greedy manner in which it was harvested. If nothing was left standing in a matter of a few years, this whole area could be a graveyard and this would be an adverse situation since it would take years for the trees to grow again to adult size. Bruno finally convinced the wealthy owner, who was not a forester of the severe outcome of what he was doing if he didn't stop now. Bruno had witnessed this many times in Italy and was paying a grievous price for this destructive procedure. One man helped preserve a small part of northern Pennsylvania's treasured forest.

Bruno and Frank cut only the largest trees, spacing them so that the smaller ones and the seedlings could grow and thrive. the logs were then tied to a huge tractor and skidded to the railroad. There they were loaded and shipped to their final destinations; a few were shipped by truck to the nearby vicinities.

Rosie thought she was very helpful when Bruno let her work the straight saw. Frank would cut a wedge into the base of the trunk on the opposite side that the tree was to be felled. Then the long five-foot straight saw with a handle on each end would be inserted into the wedge. Rosie, with Franks help, would push and pull the saw back and forth in the log until the tree was about ready to fall. Rosie had to stand way back while Frank and Bruno fell the tree. An axe and a handsaw were then used to remove the limbs and branches. The larger limbs were cut into firewood. The branches made a big bond fire.

Bruno took Rosie to see the log and coal train cross the Kinzua bridge. The bridge spanned s huge gorge 300 feet deep and over 2050 feet across. This overwhelmed her. She had never seen anything like it. The bridge crossing into Warren was big enough. Rosie thought the gorge was hell without the fire. She watched as the train moved very slowly across the span swaying back and forth with every move it made. Rosie thought for sure the logs would all tumble to the bottom of that hell—hole and the tracks would split and fall on top of them. Bruno explained to her that the bridge had been there a long time and the trains always made it across it safely. Then he told her that the Brooklyn Bridge he had been on when he came to this country was over 80 feet lower than this bridge. But not as well built in his opinion. Rosie still was not convinced that it was safe. She made Bruno promise to never go on that 'monstrous' bridge.

Summer passed by quickly. Raffaela took Rosie shopping for a new pair of shoes, socks, undies, and a new sweater. She had saved all summer so that Rosie would have what she needed for school. Frank bought her a nice lunch pail that she was proud of.

When the morning of the first day of school arrived, Rosie became very excited. She hurried to the train depot where the school bus stopped to take everyone to school in Mt Jewett. Frank gave Rosie a big hug and told her to ignore the boys. On her way to her seat, she saw a bunch of mean looking boys sitting in the back of the bus. Ignoring them like big brother told her to, she took her seat. They were snickering and started calling her bad names. At the school, Rosie met more roughnecks. They tried to trip her and called her whop girl. It hurt deeply but she held back the tears. Rosie's teacher met her and ushered to her seat. Rosie then just became a turtle. She figured that this way no one could hurt her. Things became steadily worse as the days passed by on the bus, several boys grabbed her lunch pail and dumped her lunch on the floor. The driver did nothing. Rosie went hungry. She became more withdrawn with each passing day. Being called names hurt inside, but getting punched and tripped really injured Rosie. Her dress got torn when one fat ugly roughneck grabbed it by the sash.

Rosie was put on free lunches when her teacher noticed that Rosie was not eating anything. She took it to mean that she was too poor and did not have any money for food. Rosie said nothing. Now she did not have to worry about her lunch pail anymore. It was too damaged to stay shut and it had to be tied. Now Rosie got to have real American food; fried chicken without sauce, chicken and biscuits, hamburgers, hot dogs with mustard and French fries. Dessert was yummy; cakes, jello, and pudding. Rosie loved the chicken and biscuits so much that she forgot she had gotten her second. When she went up for another serving, the cook yelled at her and told her to stop being a pig. With tears in her eyes, she went back to her seat and hid her face in shame. Her teacher came and put her hand on Rosie's shoulder and told her not to cry. She promised that she would never get yelled at again or be refused food. After that, Rosie never went back for second helping; she felt too embarrassed.

The harassing settled down until report card time. The teacher gave Rosie a pop eye and sweet pea doll for getting all A's on her report card. She had hoped that this would encourage other students to try harder. All it did was fuel teacher pet songs that included fat whop is a slop, big rose is not a rose, and if I had your face I'd make some glue. Rosie just crawled into her turtle shell and became withdrawn even more.

When the second dress had ripped by a huge ugly smelly boy; Rosie had to fess up to her father. Bruno was furious! A trip to the school was necessary. The whole school heard Bruno tell the poor teacher off. "Where was she? Did not she watch the scoundrels. My shaving strap could teach them a lesson that they would never forget. These 'sona ma bitches' better never touch my Rosie again." Rosie was so embarrassed; nothing helped. These farm boys got away with anything; later they became feared by the adults. Westline was not what Bruno had in mind for Rosie. He hated the thought of another move so soon: he had just gotten settled in his job.

Rosie got to be in the school play. Her family came to see her say, "Jack be nibble, Jack be quick, Jack jumped over the candle stick." Rosie was the candlestick. She prayed no one would fall on her. Her family was not impressed; she was not to be in another stupid play again.

Christmas in Westline was a solemn, quiet time. It had been a very snowbound winter since early November. Bruno was able to stop in Kane on his last day in the woods. The snow was getting too deep for cutting trees. Bruno picked up what he could for Christmas and enough staples to keep them going until the roads were cleared and the snow stopped. He had hoped to be able to spend Christmas day in Morrison among friends and relatives. The heavy snow the whole week before Christmas was much more than the 'T' could take. Getting stuck and stranded was too big of risk. Morrison was not a possible. Frank was able to find a small tree behind the train station. Rosie was not aware that she may only have one more chance to make a 'pricipo' with her brother. He was seventeen and the war was looming over everyone's head like a black cloud.

CHAPTER 4

The flood

Late spring of 1942, the weather became suddenly very warm. The heavy snow was melting very rapidly, crashing into every stream and river. The Kinzua Creek was threatening to go over its banks and the Alleghany River was not far behind. Every body of water no matter how small it had been was now a threat to the area. Then the rains came. It rained for over three days and nights straight. Everything became flooded for miles around. Westline was now isolated. There was not a road or bridge forgiven. All had raging waters over them. Bruno had left his 'T' at the factory. It set on higher ground than we did. He did not expect the small creek in front of the house to get as high as it did, but water was already raging everywhere. By the time he had walked back to the house on the tracks, the little house was surrounded in flooded water. Frank ran up the tracks to the factory to get the trolley, while Bruno fought with water about his waist to save the stupid pig. Frightened as it was, cooperation was not to be had. The chickens were safe because they flew to the top roasts and stayed there. Bruno hoped they could survive without food for a day until he cooked feed them. After struggling to pull that stupid beast with a rope around his neck and front legs as far as the tracks, it got loose and ran off. Bruno said several choice words that are not mentionable. He was wet, cold, tired, and hungry. He went into the house to put on dry clothes. And assured Raffaela they would be okay.

Frank was back with the trolley and two long planks he stretched from the tracks to the deck. This time no one complained that the house was too close to the tracks. The water was now a foot from the first floor. The house was elevated several feet above ground; someone new what they were doing. He helped Frank get Raffaela and Rosie onto the trolley. He then lifted all the mattresses onto the top of the big table. The rest of the items that had to be put up high were taken up to the attic where it would be out of danger. With no time left to do anymore, Bruno and Frank strained to get the trolley up the knoll and over by the neighbors that had offered to take them in. They were the only other Italian family in Westline and were delighted to have the friendship of another Italian family. By the third day, the water had receded enough to enable them to gi back home the same way they had come. The water did not go through onto the first floor, thankfully, but the basement and yard were a disaster; debris, trees, dead fish, and animals all over the place. It had a horrible stench for days. Bruno and Frank spent days cleaning the mess up and spreading lime all over. The chickens survived, but were very hungry. Bruno cleaned the cage and fed them corn. The meal had been washed away.

Fortunately the Raffaeles were survivors. They had plenty of pasta rice and beans, flour yeast and oil for the bread and cooking as well. Coffee was made weaker so that it would last longer. Rosie has canned milk and cocoa with sugar, bread was always the morning staple either toasted with just butter or a bit of jam. Bruno had a few cured sausages left yet and a wheel of cheese. He sure missed having a cow. They knew they could make it until the roads were cleared and safe to travel on.

A neighbor nearby the RR station spotted the pig and came to tell Bruno. Frank was commissioned to retrieve the dirty beast. He chased the squealing critter for six hours before he was able to lasso a noose around its fat neck, getting it to the pen was another hour. By this time Bruno returned from the factory to lend Frank a hand. Bruno would have shot it if it could not be penned. Too bad, Rosie knew it would end up going to the next home that was in the works. Rosie hated the pig. Everyone harassed her about it. No one else had a pig in Westline. She had to go back to school on Monday and wished they had moved by then.

Since the end of school was nearing, Bruno and Frank set out once again to seek work in the village of Lewis Run. A fellow worker told Bruno about this village. He thought Rosie and Raffaela would be much happier there. He said that there were several Italian families there, stores, a Catholic Church, and a school right in the village. Bruno hoped that the brickyard was hiring. Perhaps the fresh air would do him some good. Bruno was becoming more ill as the time went by. He wished he did not have so much trouble with his stomach. Both he and Frank could start work as soon as school was finished.

Traveling was still a jigsaw puzzle. The flood had now receded to a high muddy river and streams. Trees and debris of all sorts was everywhere, the road crews and corps worked long hours clearing all the windy roads. The one that lead in and out of Westline was full of ruts and stones. The 'T' made for a bumpy ride. Several bridges had succumbed to the floodwaters. The log roads were used in many cases. Getting to and from school was a trying ride for Rosie. So many detours had to be used to avoid the closed roads. Rosie was happy when the last day of school finally came. She would miss her teacher who had befriended her in so many ways. She was always kind and helpful to Rosie; a guardian in the midst of demons. But most of all, she would miss her American food. (Back to basic Italian fare.) At least she could still get her biscotti in Bradford. Lewis Run was a short six miles from Bradford. Rosie could even take the bus to town if they wanted to.

PART 3

Moving to Lewis Run

Rosie is now eight years old, a big girl for her age, and much too mature for her age. Life had turned her into a little old lady. No other child her age could do as much as Rosie did. They were still normal children playing games and having fun with friends.

Therefore, I, Rosie, am going to finish writing my story in the first person. I had also before we moved decided that I no longer wanted to be called Rosie. My name is Rose: Mary Rose Raffaele. Pronounced Ruff—fell.

A new horizon

Sticks and stones, many bruised bones.
Words that pierce the heart with sorrow,
Lost faith in the virtues of mankind
As you stumble along the road to find
A rainbow shining after the storm
There must be a place called happy home.

It's time to leave the past behind,
For a new horizon where you will find
A kindness and love that must be,
A part of humanity: just wait and see.

The time to mend your faith has come,
There's happiness waiting at every door.
The sadness, pain and lonely days,
Will become the past, and exist no more.

CHAPTER 1

Moving to Lewis Run

The time to make the move to Lewis Run had come. Bruno had rented a nice house across the tracks from the brickyard. He and Frank could walk to work in just a few minutes. It didn't take but a day to say goodbye to Westline. Raffaela had never unpacked completely from the previous move. She felt like a traveling stranger. Raffaela had told Bruno that she refused to stay in Westline and to find a job soon; either that or move back to Morrison. Since she knew that the move would be very soon, it did not take long to get ready for it. Bruno's Compare once again came with his truck. This time everything was loaded but the pig and chickens. I was hoping the pig would get lost and eaten by the wolves. No luck. Compare brought it to Lewis Run the next day. Bruno penned it in the field behind the house that had a large pen that had been used for a goat. Come November, it would be dinner anyway.

I was hopeful that this time there would be a change and I would not be harassed, how wrong I was; another revelation. I could not understand the reasoning of prejudice.

The house was a large white two story contemporary model with a large porch across the front and side of it; the rooms were very large and airy. It had a huge living room, a big square dining room, and a long kitchen that was decorated in black and white. I now had modern cupboards to put the kitchenware in, a big black stove gas stove that turned on with a knob, a sink with hot and cold water. I was totally happy until I opened the bathroom door and found to my dismay that nothing was hooked up. I ran and asked dad why. He gave me that forgiving look and explained that it was because of the sewage. He said that it was too costly to repair. I walked back into the house and went back to look at the room of my dreams again. That was exactly what it was; a dream turned into a nightmare. It irritated me to think we had to go around the back of the chicken coupe to use another stinky outside privy. If only we could at least use the big white tub for a bath I would have been satisfied; back to the small round tub. I pacified myself with the task of choosing my bedroom. Frank gave me first choice. I liked the front one because it had two windows that I could se out of. They faced the road and the brickyard. How could I miss anything? There was a large walk in closet Frank and I laughed about. He was teasing me about having enough room for my two dresses and a coat. Frank took the back room. This way he would not disturb me when he went to bed late. The middle one later became the smoke room. Mom and dad turned the living room into the biggest bedroom they had ever had. Mom could not climb stairs very well any more so this was convenient for her. We worked like beavers getting settled. I ironed the curtains. Frank hung them up for me. We only had shades for our bedrooms for the time being. But that was okay. I planned on helping mom make curtains as soon as we had enough flour sacks that matched.

CHAPTER 2

Meeting Greta

I had heard that there was a girl my age living in the house on the other side of the rubble that once was a church. It had burned to the ground and nothing was ever cleaned up afterwards. Hopefully she would be nice and come to visit me. I had been sitting on the front porch for three days when she finally walked by. I held my breath. Would she speak to me? 'Hi', she said. 'I have to go to the store for my mother. Would you like to come with me?' 'Oh I would love to.' I squeaked I was so excited; I told mom what I was doing. She asked me to get a bar of soap for washing clothes and out the door I ran. 'Sorry that I could not come sooner' she said. I had to help my mom with the baby. My name is Greta; Marguarita Thompkins. What is your name?' I answered, 'I am Rose; Mary Rose Raffaele: my first true friend; my lifetime friend.

Besides being so happy to have someone that was not a cousin or an older neighbor, I could not get over being able to walk to a store.

Lewis Run is a small village six miles south of Bradford. It sits in a valley surrounded by high hills. To my delight, it had two grocery stores, a drugstore, a gas station, and a small general store. There was a catholic church over the general store. This delighted my mother. She could at last return to practicing her faith and go to church every Sunday, besides I now could receive Holy Communion. We passed our school. As Greta put it, 'It was a two story brick building.' Everyone attended this school through eighth grade. Then they took the bus to Bradford for high school.

We got our groceries and headed back home. Greta introduced me to a couple of girls. They were polite, but very cool to me. I ignored it by now. I was used to this. At least they did not say anything nasty. I went to Greta's house after I gave mom the soap. Greta wanted me to meet her family. I could not wait to see the baby. I had never seen one this small before. Her brother Kenny was two months old. Her mom let me hold him. He was so cute and cuddly and smiled at me. Then I started to cry. I remembered that I had lost a baby brother when I was four years old. Greta's mother and grandmother consoled me and said I could hold Kenny any time that I wanted to. Greta's father worked at the brickyard with my father and they became friends. I was glad to know that.

Greta was just as poor as we were; even more so. Walter, her father, had to support four people by himself. At least both Frank and my father were bringing home a paycheck. I discovered that I was Greta's first real friend. She admitted that the other girls were snobby to her because she was poor. This gave us a bonding that was to last a lifetime, although I didn't know it then. We both loved music and would spend hours listening to songs on her grandmother's radio. We would sit behind the garage at my house and sing our heads off. We did not think anyone could hear us back there except the cows next door. On rainy days we played cards and checkers. The only games Greta had. We would go for long walks all over Lewis Run. I got to know the village as well as the back of my hand. These walks shattered some of my hopes. I had thought that harassment was a world of the past. I found that I was wrong. How could a village that had so many Italians still have people with so much hatred towards us? One maniac man Musolini stained all of our reputations. I hated him.

Greta and I did disagree on many things She had a bad temper if aggravated enough. I was as stubborn as she was about many issues. This would end up with Greta pulling my hair and yelling at me. I in turn slapped her and went home. Hurt by her actions but I was just as much at fault. The next day Greta would be at my door apologizing to me. I quickly forgave her and I off we would go for a walk. We never fought on our walks. But I did get harassed. One boy poked a stick at me and spit on my shoes. Greta tore after him with all fours. He ended up with a black eye and a bloody nose. On another day a boy named Joey, who was Italian and my mother had visited his mom, grabbed my new straw bonnet and threw in the creek a long side his house. Greta had gone to church with me that morning. Before Joey could turn and run into his house, Greta grabbed him by the nap of his neck and into the water he flew. He went to his mother to tattle. All he got after retrieving my bonnet was a soaking and told he had to stay in for the rest of the week. That pleased me. At least someone knew when a wrong had been made and tried to correct it. I could not thank Greta enough. It was one thing if she beat the tar out of me, but don't let anyone else touch me; if 'thy' knew what was good for them. At the age of nine, Greta was a very tough girl. No one in school bothered her or me any more.

One day I asked her about the neighbors on the other side of our house. She told me the Ogden's lived there. A boy named Bruce lived with them while his parents worked in Philadelphia. He lived there with his grandparents and an aunt named

Sadie. She warned me that he was a pampered spoiled boy. I still wanted to meet them so Greta took me over one day. They were all very nice to us and asked if we would like to play with Bruce. Greta said that she had to go help her mom. This meant no politely. I said I would stay if it were all right with them. They called Bruce down and I said 'my name is Rose." Would you like to do something with me?' He disappeared and came back with an arm full of games. We chose monopoly. He said he would teach me. I learned to play all his board games too well and win all the time. This would send him up to his room crying. Then I would go outside and watch his Aunt Sadie as she weeded her flowerbed. She guessed what had happened and told me to ignore him. He would get over it soon. Bruce had a pet goat called Mickey. We would dress him up and Bruce liked to pretend he was a circus animal. I went along with it. Bruce was only six years old. I didn't want to hurt his feelings. The only time I played with him was when Greta could not be with me because she had chores to do.

Saturdays was baking day at the Ogden's. His grandmother and aunt would spend all day baking for the coming week. I would watch them as they made pies, cakes, cookies bread and all sorts of rolls. I wanted to learn to bake too, so I asked them if I could watch. They said yes as long as I was quiet and stayed out of the way. Sadie got me a stool and set it along the door. 'This would be fine', she said. I would be out of Mrs. Ogden's way. Each week I would hurry over real early and sit on that stool ready to watch and learn. I decided that it would be better if I paid attention to one thing at a time and memorize everything. This was a gift I had and used it to the fullest since I never had books to read after school. As soon as that baked item came out of the oven I would hurry home and try to make it. I never new if my things were as good as theirs because they never even offered me a cookie. This perplexed me since I grew up in an environment where everyone shared and always offered you food when you were in their homes. Were we strange (or just Italian). Frank praised me on my baking. He loved the apple pie and sugar cookies best. I had a few flops, but for a ten-year-old I thought I did pretty well. Greta never got baked goods much. Her mom did not have the time and they couldn't afford the ingredients. Once she tried to make the Hershey chocolate cake, since she did not have shortening, she used bacon grease. She was nice and offered me a piece. I gagged on it, but did not want to be rude. After two bites I said that I was full and thanked her. She guessed the reason and told me that she would never use bacon grease again. I always shared my goodies with Greta. Mom was always trying to feed her because she was so thin. Greta never refused. She loved Italian food.

That summer, my dad came home with a cow. He had tied it to the back of the 'T' and walked it home from Custer City. That caused a ruckus. People thought he was being crude. Even though he drove very slowly and stopped several times to pet her and give her some grain. Well I thought here we go again. The chickens were bad enough. Now we had a cow to take care of. Thank goodness the pig was gone. I could not help liking her. She was gentle and pretty with a daisy between her ears. Yes, I named her Daisy. She was a Swiss mix and would give us lots of good milk my dad explained to me He grazed her in our backfield that was fenced in at night. He tethered her to a long pole. This had to do till he finished turning the one car garage into a stall for her. I helped Tom milk her once in a while. She never gave me a hard time, but she sure gave dad a hard time because she wanted me to do it. Now we had fresh milk every night. Dad made fresh ricotta everyday. He also made fresh basket cheese and several other varieties that had to be cured. My favorite was mozzarella and ricotta. I did not like the salty ones as much. He knew Greta did not get much milk, so he always sent some home with her, as well as a bowl of ricotta.

My parents had made several friends in Lewis Run. The Pantuso's were our favorite family. They treated us like we were a part of their family. One of the sons was a barber, so Frank and my dad got their haircuts there. Carolyn, their only daughter, was a pretty lady. I secretly wished Frank would marry her. She was such a nice person and full of fun. At last my mother was happy again. However, dad was getting sick again. He was becoming grumpy and short tempered. The doctor, Mr. Bullfrog, thought he should have surgery, but mom was not in favor of it She had undergone surgery three times and felt that the doctors were more butchers then surgeons. Dad started hitting me for the moist stupid reasons. If Greta hit me or pulled my hair he went berzurk. Then why was it all right for him to beat me with the strap after he had told me not to play with her, but I did any-how. I began to start hating him. How could he be so mean all of a sudden? Frank was hanging out with some guys that had a band and they asked him to join. Every night Frank went down

to the gas station and jammed with the guys. This irritated dad; he told Frank to stop being a bum. Frank did not listen, so dad broke his prize country guitar he had worked so hard to buy. This really angered me. I did not know what to think. Just when things started to get better for us, dad shattered our dreams.

My second year of school was starting in a week. I had mixed feelings about going since I knew that the war would put more hatred into everyone towards us Italians, Carolyn had talked to me a lot about this. Our teacher was well prepared for this situation. She was such a gem. She tried to explain to these meatheads what the war was all about and that none of us had anything to do with it. We did projects on it and it did help for some that had brains enough to learn.

My brother would be eighteen that June. We feared he would be called to service. They wasted no time; he left for the service the next week. We were devastated, I missed him so much and mom and dad were in a state of remorse and fear. He wrote every week to let us know that he was fine as long as he was in the states. He could tell us where he was. He took a few furloughs and would come home for the weekend. He was hitch hiking home from Bradford when dad drove by. Dad passed him up and then realized it was Frank. He backed all the way to pick Frank up. One day a telegram came. I thought I'd faint, I was so afraid something was wrong. Frank would be in NYC for a few days before he shipped out overseas. We could take the bus to the NYC terminal and he would meet us there to spend a day with us before he left. Many of the Morrison guys had already shipped out by now. It was a long bus ride. Mom remembered it well when she had come here from Italy. It was late at night when we arrived. We found a bench and tried to rest sitting up. The morning came; we ate our bread and cheese and waited for Frank to come at eleven o clock. We waited all day and all night. By the next morning we knew that he had been shipped out early and that there was no way to tell us. We were all in tears. I slept on the bench till our bus arrived for our return trip. Dad and mom had spent a whole day preparing Frank's favorite food that we could carry with us. The pepperoni, cheese, and butter held up okay. We had to throw out some of the chicken and meatballs.

It was two weeks before we heard from him. We were all a basket case by then worrying about him. All he could say was that he was in the Frankfort, Germany Army Base. He was assigned to the radio communications division of his platoon. Dad felt this was a little safer than some other assignments. He would be more protected from the enemy. He had been in World War One so he knew what it was about. Every night he and mom sat with the radio tuned to news of the war hoping to hear that the enemy surrendered and that it was over. That was a three—year prayer. In the meantime we would send Frank packages of pasta, sauce, pepperoni, bread, and butter. The guys would all get together on their leave days and have a feast on us. I wrote to Frank the same day his letters arrived. When Frank got my letters, the guys would gather around for him to read it out loud. I did not find this out till after he came home. I guess my wit and humor entertained them. I always tried to say things that would make Frank laugh. I would also assure him we were all fine [dad wasn't] because I didn't want him to worry. I told him to get rid of all the rats and come home soon.

Before he came home, he took a trip to Switzerland. He went to see Veronica Lake. I asked him if she was pretty just to be funny. He sent me a pink-gold watch, a green box camera, and a bracelet. A trunk arrived full of ceramic religious statues. They were slightly damaged. Some had broken hands and arms. Dad bought some glue and put them together the best he could.

CHAPTER 3

The bull

It was decided that it was time for me to prepare for first Holy Communion. Every Saturday morning I was to attend class from 10 to 11 a.m. Mom felt safe in allowing me to walk to church and back home. I was required to also attend mass every Sunday. The trips were going well. All the rough necks were in class with me looking very saintly. They did not dare misbehave. Sister used her ruler to freely.

Mom had been working on a new rose-colored suit for me. I had outgrown my blue satin dress. Mom always made sure we had one nice Sunday dress to wear. Finally she finished it and I was very happy with it. She had designed a waistline jacket and a flare skirt. I wore it the next Sunday morning.

I had noticed a big mean looking black bull tethered to a stack beside a small barn. I had ignored it; just another cow. Not so this morning! As I walked by on the way to church it started snorting;

bowing its head and pulling on the tether. I ran out of its sight as fast as I could and never stopped till I got to the church door.

Going home was a repeat of getting to church. I now became a little frightened. I told dad about him and he told me to just walk faster and not look at it.

The bull had never bothered me on Saturdays. I could not figure out what the problem was. It never even noticed me the previous Sunday. It had rained heavily the next Saturday night. Since it was still drizzling, I carried my umbrella that Sunday morning. It was red and matched my new spring coat. Now this monster of a beast really got angry. I ran all the way to church again. After classes, I was afraid to go home. I tiptoed to the bend before the bull barn. That did not work; the bull spotted me anyway. He really started doing his bull thing. He dug into the grass with his front hoofs, snorted, put his head down and started charging in my direction. I ran, maybe flew home. I had 500 feet to go to turn left onto my road and never looked back knowing that the beast had loosened the tether. I could hear it clanging on the road. It was turning into our yard as I slammed the front door shut.

Dad had seen it and was loading his high-powered rifle he used to shoot bear and deer with. 'I shoota the bastard', he was yelling. 'He never going to chasa my Rosie again." By this time the bull had knocked the railing down and ripped the steps away from the porch. He was about to fire the rifle when the bull owner came running pleading, 'Don't shoot it please! I take care of it.' Dad told him it had better never happen again or the beast would be steak and meatballs for sure.

He tried keeping it in the barn, but that did not work out. It kept breaking the door down and the neighbors complained so much he had to get rid of it.

Greta was telling her dad about my bout with the bull. 'Rosie', he said, 'That's-a-brahma bull. He was being used at small circuses. You were wearing a hot pink suit; a pretty one. I saw you with it on last week. That drives the bull mad because it gets teased with a big red cape to make it charge at it. It is called bull fighting. Usually the bull ends up getting killed by the matador as the man is called. But this is just to show people what bullfights are'.

I was quite disturbed by this. I didn't dare wear my suit to church that Sunday in case the bull was back. I walked to the bend and peeked around the bushes ready to run. The bull was not there. I hoped it really was gone for good or I would eat him in my pasta sauce. I had enough of this beast frightening me to death!

School was out and I was wondering what to do. I missed my brother so much. I wished the war would end. Monica, one of our neighbors, asked me if I would like to learn how to make crepe roses. I said I would love to. I had seen them at her house and thought that they were so beautiful. She suggested that I make a few dozen of various colors and sell them. People had asked Monica for them, but she was too busy to make them.

As a trial run, we made a dozen of various colors. I then shyly went door knocking at the homes of people that I knew. Monica said that I was to take orders and not to sell my sample flowers. The first day I got orders for six dozen. That sent mom and me to Bradford five and dime store for supplies. Mom helped me cut and curl the paper. This kept me busy for a couple of days. I set out on Saturday to deliver my orders, using mom's big vegetable basket. It had a shoulder strap and was deep enough that the roses would not fall or blow out of it. I came home with 20 dollars and orders for another eight—dozen. By the end of summer I had made over 300 hundred dollars clear on my very first business adventure. It not only kept my mind occupied and off the war, but I had been instilled with selling skills that lasted a lifetime.

CHAPTER 4

Arividerci Lewis Run

Near the end of my last year of school in Lewis Run, there was a chicken pox outbreak. Terrified by contracting it herself; my teacher made me check everyone each day. I finally ended up with a severe case of chicken pox. Everyday I soaked in cold water, padded myself dry, and applied Vicks Vaseline on the sores. It was cool, soothing, and the only ointment we had in the medicine cabinet at the time.

I got over the chicken pox and returned to school after three weeks. Greta had been bringing me my schoolwork everyday, so I had a lot of free time after school. Greta and I liked to climb on top of the flat roof of the chicken coop. We would pretend it was a stage. Our audience watched [Daisy the cow] as we sang and danced for them. Dad caught us up there one day. He warned us the roof was weak and could collapse. He told us he would break our legs if he ever found us up there again. Greta took him seriously. We didn't listen. The next day we went up there again. Then we heard the put, put of the'' coming down the road. Greta dropped her magic wand and went flying down the ladder. She ran home the back way so dad would not see her. She never looked back to see if I was all right. As I bent down to pick up my wand, my foot went through the floor of the roof. I now was the only victim to my father's punishment, but my leg was dangling over the nest of a setting hen. She starting pecking at my leg and

I was kicking and screaming at her. Then the big rooster came to her rescue and was pecking at me. I was in burning pain, but I was stuck and couldn't get out. Dad rescued me. I was waiting for the strap punishment. He said thank you to the rooster, mind you, and sent me in to clean the wounds. After that the rooster always chased me. He was a big ever-descent colored rooster and came up to my waist. Dad kept putting him in the cage, but he kept escaping. One day, he sneaked up behind me and jumped at me almost pecking at my face. Dad came running with the milk can still in his hands, threw some at the rooster, then, grabbed him by the neck. End of rooster, beginning of huge pot of soup

Dad started coming home more tired each passing day. He no longer worked at the brickyard. He was transferred to Custer City to a lighter inside job. I would take the caboose to meet him once in a while. Dad knew the engineer well and he would stop in front of our house and let me ride the three miles to Custer City. I got there one day and heard a lot of laughing and yelling at the same time. Apprehensively, I peeked in the door. Dad had tied this really fat man to a bench with a woman's girdle so that he could not get up. He had his arms inside it and all the man could do was kick his feet and yell bad words. Dad was saying 'you lazy fat son-of-a-bitcha. After the boss come and I tell him that you sleep every afternoon and let me do all the work. I will let you out'. The boss came, was told the story, the man was fired.

Dad told mom one day that he wanted to go back to Morrison. He could not take working with heavy bricks anymore. He knew he could still make charcoal. This upset me, but I resolved to the decision. Then maybe we could move to Warren in a year or so. Greta could come to visit me and I could come visit her. School ended; we left Lewis Run in June of 1945.

Greta sat for three weeks on the front porch of our house, crying and not eating. I was heartsick when I found this out. I wrote to her and promised to see her soon. I missed her very much, but I had a lot of people to keep me occupied. Greta had no one.

PART 4

CHAPTER 1

The return to Morrison

The Morrison move had been a well—rehearsed adventure. It was our third move in four years. Our house was still vacant, but it needed a good cleaning. We spent over two weeks getting things back in order. Now we were back to cold icy water and no conveniences. If it had not been for the fact that I knew the stay would be only for a few years, I would have gone out of my mind. My sentiments were still here, but Morrison was dying. On the positive side, this was still my home. I was accepted for who I was. No one ridiculed me in any way. Oh, my cousins teased me, but it was all in fun. I hoped that school would be the same.

There were seven of us girls and five boys out of the twenty-seven. I had said goodbye to. Four of the girls kept pretty much to themselves, the other three were all older then I; more like my big sisters. I spent most of my time with Ange and Sue at their house. I was always welcome and they always looked out after me.

In the evenings we would all get together, young or old, and play softball in Winold's parking lot. The exercise did me a world of good. I was no longer a roly-poly. In fact, I became too thin. I chopped off my pigtails when Jenny and Mary took me to Kinzua to the beauty parlor. I had never been in one before, so I did not know what to expect. The hairdresser thought that perhaps a perm would bring back the pretty waves I once had before mom insisted I wear pigtails. She trimmed my chopped job, washed and dried it, then started putting my hair in curlers. Then she dabbed this stinky lotion that smelled like the fluid Frank used for his furs before he hung them up to dry. He promised me it would wash out. Now, my natural curly hair was disguised in zigzag waves worse than from the pigtail waves. I ended up a frizzy mess for months. They had meant well, but in order to get rid of the mess before school started, I had to cut it real short. From then on, I cut my own hair.

We took a lot of walks on Rte 59 towards Kinzua. It was nothing for us to walk six miles to Kinzua to the grocery store . . . . there for a 5 cent Pay Day candy bar, then walk back home. We drank cool water from the many free flowing springs that were along the road. Our hands made a dandy cup. If we were lucky, we would pick berries along the way.

CHAPTER 2

The boys come home

August 14, 1945, v. j. day; the war was over! We all rejoiced with a little anxiety attached to it. Not until we heard from all the Morrison guys and a few in Warren, would we breath a sigh of relief. Soon the telegrams started coming. Everyone was coming home safe. Sam, one of Uncle Shorty's sons, had suffered from shrapnel in his leg, Nick, our neighbor, had contracted malaria. Frank was safe and sound. Thank God! Learning to shoot and hunt helped to save their lives. Toots came home with a pretty Parisan girl named Denise. What an environmental shock this was our parents and the rest of the Serrici all sympathized with her. From Paris to Morrison was as far apart as one could get. Denise could not give up her fancy shoes and fur coats. Winter came and she still wore her high-heeled toeless shoes. Finally she gave in to a pair of what she called our ugly farm boots. Toots found a job in Warren and they all moved. I missed them very much. Louie, my good-looking cousin, we had expected to come home with a blonde pretty girl. Blonde she was, but not quite what we had in mind. At least she was very nice.

Frank went to Kane shopping for the living room furniture that he had promised me during the war. He came home with a royal blue velvet sofa and matching chair, plus a wine colored lounge rocker. We now had a bedroom; living room, a little different, but who cares. I now could sit on my own plush furniture anytime I chose to. I made two embroidered pillow covers and stuffed them with downy chicken feathers. I no longer envied anyone else's living rooms. I planned on getting end tables some day to complete our family. Frank brought home a Jack Russell mix puppy. He called her Queeny. She became the best rabbit—hunting dog in the area, even though the guys teased Frank. The last laugh was on Frank. They all begged him to take their hounds out with Queeny and train them to hunt. Tom, his cat, was not too happy about the new arrival. He hissed and snarled at Queeny if she came within ten feet of him

CHAPTER 3

The Snake

As we were going on one of our usual walks, the girls decided it was too hot and wanted to turn back. I said I would go as far as Avanoli's farm for a few summer apples; then I would go back home.

As I approached the small bridge that spanned a small stream, my heart stopped. A huge rattler was curled on the road; a very rare occasion. At first I thought it was Moses, the big turtle, then I heard the warning. I froze for a moment; then backed up very slowly until I was several feet away from it. Then, I turned and ran as fast as my legs could carry me, never looking back. I knew that viper was chasing me; I had no time to look.

It was August, better known as dog days. I did not remember anyone ever saying that diamond backs rattlers did anything like this; this enormous creature was determined to attack me. I managed to stay far enough ahead of it, but I felt like I was going to faint. I starting yelling, 'Snake, snake! Don't move,' as

I passed everyone sitting on their porches. Jumping onto my porch, I pushed the door open enough for me to get through and slammed it shut. Panting, I looked out the window to see where it had gone. That slinky, ugly thing, fangs shoeing, with hatred in its eyes was curled ready to strike right outside the door. Thank God mom was not sitting on the porch just then.

Dad and mom were having lunch. I told dad about the snake and he just laughed at me. I pulled him off of the chair and dragged him to the front window. Enough said; he got his pistol aimed at the door where he thought the head might be and shot through the door. This left a hole big enough to allow him to see the viper's head. As it was ready to strike, he shot it on the head, then one more shot further down to break its neck. This left two holes in the door. He then hung the slimy thing on the clothesline for everyone to see. I ran and hid in the dining room the rest of the afternoon. Mom sat frozen in her chair in a state of shock.

The Campbell's lived in a large white house along the creek were the snake was. It is known as Campbell Run, of course. They had a black draft horse and several other farm animals. Rats were a big problem for them and they used poisoning to kill them. Dick thought perhaps the snake had gotten a hold of a poisoned rat and that drove it to insanity and made it so aggressive. He was not aware that a rattler was hanging around the farm and was quite surprised to hear about it. This made them a little more cautious about snakes and stayed on the look out for them. They could harm the animals as well as humans.

It took us three weeks before we felt safe enough to go for another walk. We had been riding anywhere we wanted to go, but Frank said it was safe to walk since the road crews had cut the grass on both sides of the road and trimmed the bushes.

As we got to Campbell Run I yelled, 'Snake on the bridge!" We all ran home yelling for Frank. We told him to get his gun, but he said no, he would run over

it with the 'T'. We all jumped in. Don't ask me why. Frank slowly eased the car to the bridge: then started laughing his head off. We uncovered our faces wondering what was so darn funny. The 'snake' was Moses, the big turtle with his head up catching every bug that was unlucky enough to fly over him. I never heard the end of that story. The guys teased me constantly about it.

Spent from all the summer's activities, we had started to settle down into a calmer environment as we waited for school to begin. There was talk about a man coming from a big city to repair the plant's chimneystack. He had been there for a few days and we did not pay much attention. It was not a girl thing. Then one day, as we were sitting in the cool back yard, we noticed all the guys running towards the back of the plant. We shrugged it off as curiosity, the boys wanted to see the man working on the chimney.

Shocked and saddened, we found out the poor man had fallen to his death. The rope became untangled and let loose. That haunted us for many months.

We hoped that no more bad things would happen. The next week we were informed by the rangers, that a little girl was missing. Would we watch out for her and report it immediately if we should see her. Everyone did more than that. All the communities banded together to form a posse. Three days later, they had resolved, to our horror; that she was never to be found. (Was she eaten by wolves or a cat?) Worse yet did she drown, never to be found; that remained a mystery forever.

CHAPTER 4

A new school again

School time was getting near. The forests were turning colors of splendid gold yellow and red. I began to marvel at the beauty of our meager home. The serenity of the cool fall days gave me an inner peace. I had resolved to living in Morrison knowing it may be the last years I would have memories of my birthplace.

We, the few that were left in Morrison, took a bus to Ludlow,

to attend school. Just as the girls promised, almost everyone there was nice. Only two out of a room of thirty-five students were worth strangling. One I almost did when he stole my war stamps and then accused me of taking his. I was still that turtle, but now I was beginning to snap. Thanks to Greta, I learned to fight back.

I met several nice girls. Mary Ann was the most helpful to me. I knew that she lived in a mansion and I never expected her to associate with me. {Her grandfather owned the tannery and half of the town] I was wrong. What a sweetheart she was; she never acted like a spoiled little rich girl. I fell in love with her; Karen Kinney road the bus with us from Red Bridge. Her father was the ranger. The three of us got along really well.

Joanne McGinney sat in front of me. We made a cozy foursome. They had all welcomed me to Ludlow. Joanne was a very talkative fun girl. Lew, as I called him, was a bit of a devil. Phil was the quiet one.

Our teacher loved artwork and made sure we got plenty of projects to do. I could not draw worth a nickel. Fruit and flowers were my limit. Lew had a bit of a problem with math. We decided to swap. He loved to draw. I loved math. We had fun helping each other out. If the teacher knew what we were doing, she never said anything to us. Since my friendship lasted only for the school day, I was still pretty much just a Morrison girl. The things they were able to do after school was beyond my reach. The bus ride home isolated me for the balance of each day. Frank and dad made charcoal at the factory now. There was not much else the plant had orders for anymore. Frank was thinking about getting a different job. I could tell dad was not well. He had become thin and very pale. His appetite was diminishing as well. We were really worried about him.

CHAPTER 5

Christmas again in Morrison

That year, Christmas was a quiet affair. With over half of Morrison gone, it just was not the same. I wondered what we doing here. Dad had come home from a doctor's visit and shopping in Warren. He announced that Uncle Joe was buying a restaurant called the Busy Bee. He had asked dad to be his chef. Mom frowned at this. She knew that he would not resist the temptation to drink wine. The doctor had told him to stay away from liquor.

The winters in Morrison were always harsh. What else could be expected at an elevation of 2376 feet above sea level? My birthday came and went. I guess eleven was not a magic number. At least spring would bless me with flowers and butterflies again.

I could not help but reminisce about my big birthday cake and party dad had for me just five years ago. It seemed like the stone age had come and gone instead. I never had or attended another birthday party again. I vowed I would always have parties for my children.

CHAPTER 6

The bus accident

It was April, but the roads were still very icy. The bus we rode was really a van equipped with two long boards, one on each side. These served as seating for us. The trip after Red Bridge was always scary to me. It was a muddy log shortcut road that cut through the high hills with an incline on our left and a steep decline on our right. At the bottom of this ravine was a creek. The road was a six-mile uphill climb all the way to Ludlow.

We had barely climbed a mile of it, when the bus started to slide and slipped back. It turned sideways, slipped back again, and came to a stop with a thud. We all dropped to the floor, terrified to look out. Calmly, the bus driver instructed us to very slowly walk out from the back to the front of the bus, one at a time. We really had the urge to run, but we knew better. Karen and I were in the middle. I let her go first.

Once out, we all made the sign of the cross and said 'thank you lord' for saving us. A huge log that had fallen off of a log truck was stuck in the ice against a large rock at the side of the road. The ravine was 600 hundred feet straight down to the creek. The log saved our lives. I could not help but wonder if it had fallen off of cousin Louie's truck earlier that morning.

One of the guys offered to walk to a cabin and ask for help. We were all huddled in the middle of the road to keep each other warm. It was a very cold windy morning. Karen wanted me to walk back to her house with her. She could have her dad or mom get help for us. On the way back to her house, we decided that we were not going to school that day. Her dad drove back up to check on the bus. Someone had already pushed it back on the road. It was on its way to Ludlow. I called Frank at the Winold's house. It was the only phone in Morrison. Edith ran and got Frank to the phone. All I said was come and get me at Red Bridge. The bus is stuck in the mud. I helped Karen feed the wild animals while I waited for Frank. Her dad retrieved orphaned and injured animals. He would nurse them back to health and then release them.

Gratefully, that weekend was a spring thaw. I returned to school but was frightened as usual when we got to the mud road. I always held my breath and sighed in relief as soon as the oil tanks appeared. I knew we would be safe then on the cement street that took us up to our school.

CHAPTER 7

Story time

We spent that summer as in past summers. The garden was much smaller than in past years. Weeding was a lot less of a hassle for all of us,. We were just biding our time till we had to move. To keep us occupied, Compare John Tassone would tell us his famous Serre fables every Friday night. We would gather around his stool for an hour of his Serre tales of where wolves with foot long fangs that ate you in one bite. Creatures that became familiar dinosaurs in future years and the powerful witch of Serra San Bruno woods that swept you away with her big broom. I never believed any of it. The girls would be so scared and entranced by these tales that they then were afraid to walk home. I ended walking them the whole 200 feet home every week. I kept telling them no creature from the Serre would be so stupid and come to Morrison. The next Friday night, they would do it again. It was just something to do.

The guys used to have top spinning contests. They all hand carved wooden tops that would 'sing' as they spun. Each would compete against one another. The one who's top spun the longest was the winner. They had fun and we cheered them on.

More events

In the summertime the running water in the houses became warm and acquired a metallic taste to it. We all would take turns going to the spring for cold water. It came rushing down the hillside in a pipe that came from a mountain spring. This was about 500 feet above the schoolhouse. We would all fill our jugs; take a big drink, and splash water on our faces. There were the remains of what appeared to have been a small cabin. It had burned down to the stone foundation and deserted. There was still the railing leading from the road to the front door and a collapsed out house in the back. On the side of the house by what once was a well, stood a huge lilac bush, always full of blooms in the early part of may, we would pick large bouquets of these and take them home to our mothers. Then, beginning in June we would pick beautiful roses that rambled from the front of the foundation to the road. We still filled all our jugs at every visit there. The mailbox was a bit tipsy, but still in tack. We had no idea of the significance of the people that once had lived there. The name was J. Neily. We found out that he was the founder of Neilyville and the beginning of our humble existence now known as Morrison. This Edith told us when we became curious and asked her about it.

The wildcat—sixth grade

My last year in Ludlow was sixth grade.(2.13) I had found a niche there by now and stayed with it. I only recall a day in the fall when Karen, Mary Ann and I decided to climb up the hillside behind the schoolhouse. Mary Ann brown bagged for the day so that she could join Karen and me for lunch. Normally Mary Ann would go home for lunch we decided to have a picnic up the hill. No one ever told us we could not go up to the rocks behind the schoolhouse. We found a group of very large rocks and decided that it was a good spot to spread out our lunches. We no sooner got ready to eat and we heard a hiss and several growls. Mary Ann was the only one that knew what it was. 'Run', she yelled as she started down the hill, leaving her lunch behind. Karen and I did not ask questions, we just got up and ran as fast as we could. Mary Ann stopped at the swing set panting. 'What was that?', I asked her. It sounded like a mad cat to me. 'A wildcat', Mary Ann blurted out trying to catch her breath. Lesson learned; we never tried that adventure again. We went hungry that day. Spaghetti never tasted so good as it did that night. We were sure the cat enjoyed our lunches.

The situations at home were not so passive. Dad was beginning to get steadily worse. He was always in great pain. Everything he tried to eat bothered him. Another trip to the doctor meant stomach medicine and more aspirin. He lived on briochi to settle his pain, but it did very little to relieve his discomfort. We knew he had something seriously wrong. Back then, if you were Italian, with a language barrier, you chose an Italian doctor with whom you could converse your problems to. I despised the fat pig faced doctor. He pilfered money out of every patient that entered his threshold. Finally, he convinced dad to have surgery against our wishes. I wanted him to go see someone else, but he refused to do so. Dad never recovered. He lay in the hospital bed, heavily sedated. He could not eat solid foods and drank very little. I knew he was going to die. He passed away on November 29th at 2:20 pm while I was over town to get a pair of socks. Mom knew he was about to go and did not want me there to see him die.

Mom was a basket case. With me to raze: what was she going to do? Certainly she could not expect Frank to support us forever. He should find a nice girl and get married.

Dad was brought to me the last time. The living room was vacated and turned into a funeral parlor for two days. Mom and several of my aunts stood vigil the whole time. Mom must have known what was to happen. She pulled a black dress out of the trunk and wore it plus one more she made for two years to mourn her loss.

We made it our last winter in Morrison in quiet sadness. Christmas was a painfully hard day for us. Comare Camilla invited us for dinner or I am sure it would otherwise have been very meager and solemn. We could not consider buying a home and relocating until the wills were executed. With Italy involved, it meant a lot of correspondence to Uncle Francesco, mom's brother. He had been named power of attorney for everything in Serre. The villa, against my wishes was up for sale. Uncle 'Cheech' as we called him purchased mom's cottage for himself. The bank had to have all the papers finalized in order for us to draw money out of our accounts that dad had set up for us. Mail took two weeks each way. The process was very slow.

Frank's money was running out. Mom's social security was still tied up in government red tape. There was not much left to do in Morrison, but we had to wait for spring to come to move

My birthday came and passed. It was just a forgotten day. Easter came and went. We hardly noticed except for the fact that mom insisted we go to church. I kept my school grades up through it all. On the last day of school, I said my farewells to all those that had befriended me. Over all my two years in Ludlow had been very pleasurable. With the exception of my two favorite enemies, I had enjoyed all my classmates. I was going to miss them. Especially Mary Ann, Karen, Lew and Phil.

The little schoolhouse on the hillside would, after this year, become a vacant silhouette with many memories. Everyone was to be bused to Kane beginning next fall. Karen stayed at Red

Bridge until the last moment. They were getting ousted. Red Bridge, the home of the CCS, was to become history. Men had already come to our house to tell us the details of the upcoming plans for a huge reservoir that would prevent any more flooding. Morrison was being acquired for a part of the dam and would be a focal point in the project. Besides Morrison, Kinzua, Corydon, Red Bridge, and many other places I cannot remember, would also be under water. We had a choice; buy the house we lived in for 5500 dollars, then have it moved at our expense to a lot we purchased, or just leave. I held my breath. I hated that house. I wanted a nice house in Warren with modern conveniences. Frank said, 'no thanks, we will leave.' Everyone was getting uprooted with little compensation. I had no idea of the scope of destruction this reservoir they were going to call the Kinzua Dam was going to be in order to prevent flooding.

Frank and mom started house hunting and found a nice house near Holy Redeemer Church just like mom wanted. Frank promised me to take me to see it. He said I would be very happy with it. I could walk to school and not put up with busing ever again. We could walk to town if we wanted to, although there was busing available.

Frank kept his promise and let me go with mom and him on the day that they were to sign the papers. I was very pleased with the house, except that I wished that I did not have to share a room with mom. I wanted my own bedroom, but I guess I could not have everything. It was a duplex and the upstairs was rented out. This would help with the mortgage payments.

Frank and I had pooled our inheritance money together, along with some of moms meager savings by Italian honor, she made Frank promise that one half of the house was to always remain mine whether we chose to keep it or sell it. I never saw a penny of it. An overpowering force conned Frank right out of it. He was not given any choice. All moneys went to the wrong undeserving place. I miss my first real home. It meant a lot to me. I revel in the memories that it gave me. That is worth more than any greenback that slips swiftly through the fingers. That said; I resume my story.

This goes after [my birthday came etc, Easter etc, we went to church}

The flood of May 27ᵗʰ, 1947

Since I had received first Holy Communion in Lewis run, I should have been going for confirmation classes according to the catholic faith. Mary and Sue were attending classes every Saturday. They asked me if I would like to go. That way I would have a head start when we moved to Warren. Nick, Mary's brother had been driving them to Kane up to now. Frank offered to take turns.

This would be my first year. Mary and Sue had already attended for a year. Since the winter driving had been so bad, we started in March. Then we could finish our classes in Warren when the time came. March and April driving was a usual 'winter driving' experience. There was still snow in the mountains by mid May; the last week of May, it started raining heavy. It just never seemed to want to stop. Saturday it was just drizzling. Frank knew the waters were high, but felt it was safe to go. We hated to miss our last day of class. The waters had risen more than Frank had anticipated, but he did not think that they would go much higher that day.

As soon as our classes were over we headed for home. He had heard rumors that Red Bridge was near flood stage. It was beyond flood stage. We had to turn back to Kane and catch Route 6 to Warren. That way we could catch Route 59 and turn back to Morrison.

Frank spent his last 5.00 dollars on gas and a snack for us in Warren. By now, we all started getting nervous. Warren's west end was becoming a lake. The banks of the Alleghany were over the flood level.

Since water was already on the road in several places, Frank drove cautiously. Gratefully the 'T's' bottom was at least ten inches from the ground. Truck tires were a bonus also. We got to devil's elbow bridge. The water was lopping almost even with the bridge road. Frank had a tense look and tight lips. It told me he was worried. He took a deep breath and told us to stay still, put the 'T' in second gear and slowly started crossing. It felt like an eternity before we got to the other side. Actually the bridge was about a100 foot span of wooden planking. It had taken us only a few minutes to cross it.

As soon as we entered 'terra firma', we broke into tears of joy and hugged each other. We all gave Frank a big hug and said thank you. He then carefully proceeded towards Morrison. We still had to watch for water and rocks across the road. Suddenly, we heard the most horrible crashing, thudding, and splashing behind us. Frank stopped. He looked like a stone statue. 'Frank', I asked, 'what was that?' 'Bobo', he said, 'I think that was the bridge going into the water.' We all said 'oh my god' in chorus. No one wanted to go back to look.

The only other bridge to cross was my critter bridge. That was only about 20 feet across Campbell run. The water had barely reached the railway tracks in Morrison. Since the houses set across the railroad and the highway, no one was aware of the seriousness of the situation. 'Just another flood.' Mom wondered why we were so late. I told her classes lasted longer because it was our last day. She did not need to know what had taken place. Life had placed enough of a burden on her shoulders. Some mouths just cannot stay shut. She eventually found out, but did not take it as hard. We were, after all, safe.

Now more than ever the making of the reservoir was re-affirmed. The loss and damage that flood created had caused destruction from New York State to the end of Pennsylvania. Pittsburgh was in a state of disaster with millions of dollars in damages and losses.

We now had to drive to Kane on the old log road and then back to Warren. Route 59 was closed from Kinzua to Kane for a long time. We all shared food and trips to keep us going.

PART 5

CHAPTER 1

Warren at last

B y now we were all 'professional' movers. Frank rented a truck for the move. Mom and I had every thing packed and ready to go. I carefully covered the living room furniture with old sheets and taped on to stay in place.

'Arivaderci Morrusono.' We were ready to go at last. The only missing element was dad. That saddened all of us. We said our goodbyes to the remaining families there. By the end of summer, they would also make the move to Warren. No one wanted the company houses, so as soon as each one found the house of their dreams, they would be in Warren.

Jeff drove the 'T' to Warren then Frank drove him back to Morrison. I had started to unload as much of the truck as I could. Some things were too heavy for me. I needed my brother's help. By suppertime we had carried the last of our belongings into the house. Miracle of miracles, I had the pleasure of my own inside bathroom; a toilet that flushed, a big bathtub, and a sink with hot and cold water. The kitchen had a white gas stove and large oven. No more charcoal for cooking and 'oh my gosh', a real electric refrigerator with ice trays. Then Frank teased me and said I had to 'defrost' it every week. I did not believe him, but it was true. It was a small price for the conveniences we would have.

As usual mom had made a pot of chicken soup for the evening meal. Frank went to Walkers and got ice cream for dessert. They were only four blocks away. That could mean trouble. I loved the ice cream.

Franks first priority was to remove one inch of wallpaper off of all the walls. The top layers were all soiled, and no more paper could be pasted over them. My wish was to paint the plastered walls with pretty pastel paint. We rented an electric steamer. Water was inserted in a barrel-like container. A hose was attached to it and a flat large iron one foot by eight inches that had a large handle finished the miracle tool. The trick was to get the paper wet by holding the steam iron on the paper for one minute and the paper would miraculously peel right off. Just like down town, 'ha ha.' It took us a week of constant working from morning till night to remove bushels of dirty wet smelly paper in four rooms. The kitchen was to be done at a later date. We sanded the crude plaster as smooth as possible and applied a sealer over it. The smell could knock one over a mile away it was so bad. Finally, we applied a base coat and two coats of candle light paint in the living room and dining room. Frank chose blue and mom liked the mint green. The floors were of mahogany hardwood that was stained with a very dark color I did not like. We bought the largest linoleum we could find and covered most of the flooring with it. Our sofa and chairs looked very minute in such a large area. At least it was a start. I had a living room. We used dads large table for the dining room. Mom and I went shopping at Warren's two big second hand stores while my brother went job hunting.

We had very limited funds for what we needed. We managed to barter for a kitchen table, four chairs, a china cabinet, buffet, and one small end table for 100 dollars. Dad had taught me well how to get a bargain. The storeowner was in disbelief when he asked my age and I said thirteen. I had grown to my lifetime five—foot—two inches and dressed much older than I should have.

I was taking a break before I hung curtains. I went out and sat on the front porch steps of 17 Plum street; happy to be in Warren. I knew that there was a girl my age across the street and hoped to become friends with her. She came out her door and looked over and saw me. Down the steps she went and across the street towards me. It reminded me somewhat of Greta and I starting missing her. "Hi", she said, I've been trying to get over here to meet you, but you seemed so busy getting settled. My name is Betty Ann Simko." "My name is Rose Raffaele. I am so glad you came over. 'I have been anxious to meet you"; my second life—time friend. We chatted for a while. She briefed me on Beaty Jr. High and promised to introduce me to her other friends

She invited me to her house the next day to meet her mom and brother, Dave. Her dad was working. Betty Ann had talked to Beverly Siden. She was to come down to Betty Ann's house after lunch. She said she would like to meet me; she was very friendly and kind. I hoped that she liked me. A little at a time, I got to meet the rest of the south street gang as they called themselves. Bette Gayle lived past my ice cream shop. She was a lot of fun but I did not see her much. Arlene and Dorothy lived on the same street a bit apart. We did get together a few times before school. That was coming sooner than we wished for. On one of our get-togethers, I told the girls that I wished I had a pair of jeans like they had, but we could not afford them right now. That's all it took. They pooled together and bought me a pair. It did not take me long to put on the jeans and slip the skirt off over my feet. My shoes were quite worn out so mom managed to buy me a pair of saddle shoes. Now I felt more like I fit in and not a spectacle. Then I wanted to learn to ride a bike. After a few spills on the tarred road, I managed to learn to stay on. After a week of practice, I felt I could join the girls for a bike adventure. I got home tired, sore but happy. The exercise and friendship did me a world of good.

Frank finally got hired at Phoenix Furniture Factory. The pay was not as much as frank would have liked it to be, but it was a job and very much needed. His trapping funds had pretty well diminished by now; there had not been time to establish a trapping route in warren area. Mom's 36dollar S.S. check helped with the groceries and at that on a strict shopping budget. Since mom was not able to do any heavy chores, I did these tasks myself. She was kept occupied with sewing my school wardrobe. I helped wherever I could. I was happy to have two skirts, three blouses, and a vest.

Betty Ann came to get me the first day of school. Compared to the small country schools I attended, Beaty Junior High was very large. I was overwhelmed as I entered the threshold that memorable day. Betty Ann and I parted at the door. Not only did we have different homerooms, we would not see each other in any of our classes. I was on my own; I was apprehensive as I found each class that day. I could not get used to having to change teachers each time. This I found later was really to my advantage. Each one had a special talent to share with all of the students that one person could not possibly execute. I accidentally was assigned to 8th grade choir. The instructor was perplexed and did not know what to do about it. She did not discover it for several weeks. By then I had pleased her with my natural gift of music that she did not want to lose me. I was the only contralto in the choir; my heart fell. I did not want to lose my choir class. It was my top reason for really loving school. Somehow, she managed to keep me. Thanks to her, I stayed in her choir until I went to high school. Then I was automatically expected in a cappella. I have never forgotten her kindness and understanding. School would never have been as joyous without my music.

Our first assembly was just before Thanksgiving break. The drama club that I was a member of had a short play on the Pilgrim's first Thanksgiving.

CHAPTER 2

'Thanksgiving break'

By the time Thanksgiving break had arrived, I was beginning to piece together the meaning of the celebration; that the pilgrims celebrated and gave thanks with a feast of a big wild turkey, venison and all the trimmings, was not unfamiliar to me. However, I, the isolated country Italian girl, did not realize that it was celebrated by everyone in the U.S. Certainly not everyone could be so fortunate as to bag a turkey for the event. Finally I got brave enough to ask Betty Ann about it. She explained everything to me including the pumpkin pie.

That night I talked to Frank about it. "Bobo, I'm sorry," he said, "I thought you knew about it. Tell you what; tomorrow we will go to the A & P shopping for our dinner. Do you think you can cook it for us? I will help you. You bet I could; at least I would try. As he entered the door that night after work, I started singing our assembly song; only my version I sang; "over the river to A & P we go, the 'T' knows the way the turkeys fly and we'll make pumpkin pie." He laughed heartily at my funny song. We were off to our adventurous shopping spree as soon as he had changed his clothes. Mom was worried we would spend too much. Frank told her not to worry; he had saved for it.

We bought a huge turkey, potatoes, peas, cranberry sauce, a can of pumpkin and a loaf of stuffing bread. I spotted a pamphlet with the title, 'how to cook the best Thanksgiving dinner.' Frank bought it for me. Armed with our feast supplies, we then wondered where to start. The day before, I decided to make the pies, the rolls, and mix the stuffing. That went well. I could not keep Frank out of the pies he snitched a piece of it liking it too well. Thanksgiving morning, Frank cleaned the bird for me and I stuffed it. We put all the spices on it, poured apple juice over it, and baked it as instructed. The rest of the meal was familiar to me. I left a few potatoes plain for mom. The rest I mashed. My lumpy gravy was put through a strainer and saved; Frank was supposed to be watching it. He was too busy sampling turkey and forgot. We had a lot of laughs; one blamed the other for the mistakes. All in all the meal was pretty good. Mom was impressed. I vowed to buy a few cookbooks with my spare babysitting money before Christmas arrived.

As I lay in bed that night, the events of the day kept flashing in my head. Just think, I had not only prepared an American dinner; I got to eat it! My early childhood dreams had come true. I was beginning to feel like I belonged and would not be looked upon as weird. I had so much to learn about the American ways. The better part of me was still Serrici with isolated traditions and beliefs. I tried to hide my ignorance as much as I could, but I'm sure a lot of it showed. I had made a few friends, but I never felt like I truly belonged. Surely they must have thought me strange. I vowed to keep my eyes and ears open to everything my classmates did.

It was hard getting up early on Monday morning. I pulled the shade up to a panoramic view of fresh fallen snow; another day of wet feet This time I remembered to put a second pair of socks in my coat pocket to change out. I walked over to meet Betty

Ann. We started telling each other about our feast, when a few of the other girls met up with us. The conversation turned to 'how was Thanksgiving?' I listened as each one gave their account of the day. One of the girls stopped walking. 'Oh no Rose; were sorry; we should not be talking this way. You probably did not have a regular Thanksgiving dinner.' I was surprised that they knew so much. Did I show my ignorance that much. 'Oh but you are wrong. We had a very good dinner. Frank helped me to cook it.' They could not believe this, I was sure. It did not matter I was happy and proud of Frank's and my accomplishments; it gave me a feeling of belonging.

The next two weeks were filled with Christmas events. Our choir was to perform at the high school for a joint assembly. The parents were invited. I was both excited and nervous. What if I sang off key or forgot the words? Then I thought that if I sang very softly no one would notice. I got caught and was prompted to sing louder. All my worries were in vain. The assembly went very well. I was saddened that I had no one of my family to see me. Frank was working late and mom could not walk that far.

Seven of my choir friends and I decided to go Christmas caroling. We got together at Fran's house to practice. She lived more or less in the center of town. We had a lot of fun together, but we could not believe the way we were ignored. No one even as opened their' doors to thank or cheer us. We gave that idea up the second night. With exams looming over our heads, we did not feel like wasting our time.

With two weeks Christmas holiday ahead of us, we all had busy plans for each day. I worked most of the time every day after school and on weekends. I was asked to help during the day if I could. The time slipped by quickly. Christmas Eve came too soon. I was unprepared for the impact of Christmas without dad. We had no one to share our goodwill with. Morrison was dead. Everyone slipped into their own cacoon once they hit

Warren. Without dad there were no cheeses he had proudly made, no wine to taste and boast about, no prickly pears, and no one to share our bounty with. The three of us had a quiet chicken dinner. The only thing that glittered was a very small tree without the orecipio under it. Frank gave up putting the manager under the tree. It was his way of mourning dad. Mom bought me a brown and green plaid winter coat. It only had one big button at the top. A New Process special for 15 dollars; more than mom should have spent. Frank surprised me with a jewelry box he made for me at work. I got mom a warm sweater and my brother a new hunting cap.

I missed the New Year's Eve get-togethers we had in Morrison. The pizza, wine, eggnog, cookies and Italian ice. But mostly, I missed our comradeship, the tarantella, polkas, and sing a longs we shared. I was saddened to think Morrison would no longer exist on terra firma; just a buried memory that I vowed no one would ever take away from me. I was glad to be in Warren, but I wished that at least a part of my past could have stayed with me

School resumed; a new year beckoned me to excel. I buried myself in my schoolwork and was rewarded with honor roll grades. 'Compare' Mike kept a close watch on me; honor students were published in the Times. I missed it once. It was not but a day and 'Compare' Mike was at our door. It did not take him long after his polite greetings to ask me about my report card. After I explained to him that my gym teacher gave C's if you did not take a shower. The reason I did not he was appeased, but angry with. I knew she would hear about it. I had contacted athlete's foot in the dirty shower stalls. My doctor told me to stay out of them or I would never get rid of the sores. My gym teacher would not honor that request. Gratefully, she was removed and a new nice teacher took her place. No more bad grades.

Spring was promising to come and we felt it was not soon enough. It had been a sloppy winter with rain and slushy snow mix for the whole month of March. I was aware of Easter's coming arrival because we were preparing a special mass for that day. I had joined Holy Redeemer's choir before Christmas but did not sing in it for the holiday; for the three of us it was just another day. We had our usual chicken dinner that we had every Sunday. I made mom's biscotti and a pie for Frank. I was too big for an Easter basket anymore. 'Compare' Mike still showed up with a big chocolate Easter egg. At least someone remembered us.

This time I was grateful for Monday morning. I thrived on my school activities and work schedule. Mom went to mass every morning. She made friends with an Italian lady that lived near by. I was happy to see she had found companionship at last. She stayed busy baking bread and cooking. It kept her from getting depressed. Frank was in seventh heaven. Fishing season was starting next week. No more fish anytime Morrison style. He had to get a license and follow the rules. We were free range in Morrison. The ranger seldom had time to check on the Morrison boys. Gratefully, we survived on them and all the other game.

My first year at Beaty was coming to a close. I had completed a milestone in my life there the past nine months. I still had a long ways to go and a lot more to learn. It was a get acquainted year for me. It would take me time to feel welcomed and a part of the classmates. They all spoke to me, but I was never included in any of their parties or activities. I missed Greta very much, even though Betty Ann and I had become good friends. I had been more welcomed in Ludlow than here and I missed them as well. I vowed to work harder on this endeavor. Next year would be easier.

Frank and I scraped and painted the house. We kept it white and changed the trim to forest green. We also put a small garden in. We had very limited space. I could almost hand my neighbor a cup of coffee we were so close. I had saved the pits from some white peaches we had purchased last fall. I also saved the pits from the Italian plums Uncle Shorty had given us. I carefully turned the soil and dug a hole and set three pits into it. Then I used some fertilizer, watered them, and covered them completely. Frank just chuckled and told me not to hold my breath. He did not think I would ever see a tree come from either of the seedlings. 'Ha' surprise! Both came through. It took a while, but I never gave up hope. I nurtured them to full-grown trees that bore the best tasting peaches ever and the biggest plums Frank ever ate. Guess he stuck his foot in his mouth that time. He never doubted after that when I said I was going to grow something. I planted mom a beautiful pink rose bush from a bloom she brought home from her friend's house. These things kept me busy and gave me a feeling of worthiness.

CHAPTER 3

Warren's first Fourth of July parade

Everywhere I went, people were talking about the big festivities that the Jaycee's were planning for Warren on the Fourth of July. I could hardly wait for the time to come. This was going to be my first experience with another unknown holiday to me. The isolation of Morrison, the ethnic way of life I knew, was no match for what I was about to have unveiled. Perhaps other members of the Morrison community have a previous opportunity for all this, but I believe originally we were all in the same situation. Word of mouth educated many a Morrisonite before they ever left the village. Some of us were too young to understand the meaning of many things.

The day finally arrived. Betty Ann and I walked to the Pennsylvania Avenue Bridge that spanned the Conewango Creek and picked our spot. We had two hours to wait for parade time, but we got the prime spot we wanted. We passed the time away chatting with people as they passed by. The bridge filled up early. It was supposed to be where everyone stopped to perform. Finally, we could hear the beat of the drums as the band was marching onto the avenue. I could almost hear my heart keeping pace with them. The first float came by; it was so beautiful. A lot of work went into it; it was covered with red roses,. I wished I could have donated some of my time. I could have made the roses with a little help; maybe next year. For an hour we watched as one spectacular float went by after another. In between were great bands, cars, fire trucks, and may local groups marching. I could not digest all that I witnessed for the first time in my life.

That afternoon, we went to memorial field to watch the band competition. Every band that had marched in the parade was to perform for thirty minutes. They were to be judged on their drills, music, style, and appearance. I had a hard time picking my favorite one. They were all great as far as I was concerned. Then that night we went to Beaty field and sat on the ground to watch the fire works. They thrilled me as each one went up and burst into a panorama of beautiful colors and design. We hated to see them come to an end so soon.

The rest of the summer went by slowly. I was babysitting as much as possible to earn money to buy the things we needed. I felt like I should do my share. 25 cents an hour did not add up very fast as far as I was concerned, but a dollar a night was better than empty pockets.

Betty Ann, a few of the other girls, and I went for bike rides. This always included a picnic lunch and swimming. Swimming for me meant an inner tube. We had to carry it on my bike. It helped me to hover close to the banks of the water. For being a Pisces, I sure was a big scary cat of the water. Swimming was out of limits to me in Morrison. Everyone went to a big hole on Campbell run. We had to walk through high grass, with a stick to clear the way. No one lived in the pine cottage on the other side of the run, so the grass was never mowed. I was too afraid to go after Jerry Defabio was bitten by a rattler. Lucky for him, Toots was there and knew what to do.

I was sitting two girls that were almost too old to be watched. Lucy, their mother, felt safer when her and Harry, her husband, went out for an evening. Her brother and sister-in-law lived across the street from them. They had four young children under five and Mary was expecting her fifth one. She needed someone that could handle four kids. Lucy felt I was capable of this task. I was asked to baby sit the following weekend. When I got there, the kids had all been put to bed. I was just to check on them occasionally to make sure they were covered and safe. There was a stack of dishes in the sink, so I washed them, but did not attempt to put them away. Then I went upstairs to check on my little strangers. They were all fine. As I started down the steps, I noticed a huge basket of clothes that needed ironing. I took this down to the kitchen and looked for the iron and board, I was bored with nothing to do and thought this may help Mary if I ironed as much as possible. I had to dampen a lot of them and let them set in a towel for a while. I was surprised to discover that Mary, with as much as she had to do, ironed everything including dishtowels and pillowcases. I gave them a quick going over. They did not seem important enough to fuss over. Then I ironed Tony's shirt and pants, Mary's dresses and started on the kid's clothes. The girl had frilly dresses with sleeves that challenged any professional presser. I did the best I could. They came home a little while after I had taken the clothes back up stairs and checked on the four sleeping angels again. I planned to come visit them so I would know whom I was watching. Mary asked me to baby-sit the next day. She had a doctor's appointment. I said I would be glad to. When I got there, Mary had a bewildered look on her face. I was afraid I had done something terribly wrong. After saying hello, Mary asked me who came and ironed the clothes last night. Rose, I had told you not to have anyone here while we were gone. With a sigh of relief I answered, 'I did not have anyone here. I washed the dishes, sorry I did nit put them away.' Then I saw the basket of clothes as I was coming down the steps; I had gone up to check on the kids. I was bored with nothing to do, so I ironed them for you. Sorry if I did something I was not supposed to do. She could not believe it! 'How could a thirteen-year-old iron shirts so perfectly?' Tony was impressed. I just shrugged and said, 'I have been ironing my brother's shirts for the past three years. It was no problem.' She had a neighbor girl that came in to help with the cleaning. She would wipe around the edges of the furniture and mop only the part of the floors that showed. Before Mary returned from her appointment, I had dusted the downstairs and mopped all the floors, this really sent Mary and Tony into a state of shock. She was so impressed that she asked if I would also help her with the weekend cleaning; of course I would. I finally got a job. The next time I babysat, Mary was worried she would not be back in time to cook dinner. I told her not to worry, but she did not understand what I meant. She had planned on making spaghetti sauce. This I knew I could do with my eyes shut. When she walked into the kitchen, she said, 'Oh my God, I don't believe this. Rose, did you cook this?' Well of course I did. Marie helped me find everything and the twins, Molly and Patty watched. Phillip was not interested. He had his toys to play with. To make a long six—year story short, I ended up being the babysitter, cleaning lady, occasional cook, hairdresser, and whatever else had needed to be done. They had purchased a large white house across the street. Soon after Jimmy, the baby was born. This was sometimes more than I could keep up with. I loved the kids; they were all so adorable and well behaved, except for Phil. He was my pickle. I guessed he did not like me; or my authority. I caught him trying to sneak out the door with a sleeve of crackers to share with his friends. He was told not to do thus. I grabbed the door and held it shut. He was so mad that he charged at it putting his arm through the glass. This rewarded him with several cuts on his arm. Crying and kicking, I washed the cuts, put a disinfectant on them, and bandaged them. Well, I thought; 'there goes your job, Rose.' Quite the contrary, I was thanked for what I did; Phillip was grounded for a week. I stayed with the Orioles until I graduated and took a full time job. They became like my family, I loved them all; even Father Phillip. It would take another book to tell all the things that I experienced during my tenure at the Oriole kingdom. I shall put it to rest in my memories for now, as I must return to Beaty to continue my saga apart from my life with the Orioles

As a short recollection, I had finished seventh grade and passing the summer away waiting for my second year at Beaty. Eighth grade was to be a steppingstone towards high school. I did not have much choice on the subjects I wanted. However, English and math still remained my favorites. Frank's old girl friend from Lewis Run ended up being my most dreaded class; art. She asked to bring a bar of ivory soap to class. We were to carve an animal out of it. I tried to carve a duck. How hard can that be? When I went up to hand it to her she said, 'Rose, why did you choose a dodo bird?' My heart sunk. That did it. I vowed to never attempt to do anymore art work. I had to stay in the class. It foolishly was a required subject then. Out of sympathy, she gave me C's the rest of the year. I was glad that I had known her, or I certainly would have flunked.

Eighth grade was a big step up for all of us. We were preparing for that big era of scholastic standing called high school. We were kept busy with homework every night. This drove Betty Ann insane. She hated carrying all those books every day. I had to get mine done during study hall and lunch break. With the work schedule I had, there was not much time for anything else, let alone homework.

We finally got a holiday break for Thanksgiving. The weather had turned very cold. Fall seemed to just disappear and give in to a slushy, snowy November. Without any boots, my feet were always cold and wet.

We had our second Thanksgiving; even better than the first one. Frank had gone turkey hunting with his friend, Don. Frank bagged a 20 lb turkey. This delighted me until I got stuck cleaning the ugly thing; entrails and feathers. Once cleaned, I did not think about how it looked before. I was too busy planning on how to prepare it. Since I now was armed with a small cooking library, I did not think it would be a problem cooking this type of bird. What I found was not enough to do what I planned to do. Tossing the book on the shelf, I decided to rough it. Frank thought I should skin the whole thing. I felt this would dry it up, so I pulled the skin away and tucked all the spices and melted butter under it. Then I poured apple juice over it. It baked better than a store bought one and made the best gravy. No more soup; only wild turkeys. We had a great feast once again.

CHAPTER 4

An unexpected change

Frank and I would go visit everyone at uncle Shorty's house. It became a magnet-like gathering place in Warren just as it had been in Morrison. There were two girls that started coming the same nights we were there. Both had the same name; Rose. That became very confusing. When someone was addressing a Rose, none of us dared to answer until we found out which one of us they were referring to. I began to think that this was not a coincidence. I finally woke up to the fact that they both were trying to get my brother's favor. Neither one impressed me. He had dated so many other nice pretty girls in the past; I thought he would ignore them. I was so wrong. One rose finally won out. The relationship grew into an engagement.

Christmas now became a different day for both mom and me. I could tell she was not pleased with Frank's choice. Mothers never think anyone is good enough for their darlings. Her parents invited us to Christmas dinner her mother was a great cook. But her bragging could have been kept in a closet. Mom did not enjoy herself at all. I was glad when Frank finally took us home. We still missed dad and his traditional holidays.

With Christmas break over, we resumed the final leg of eighth grade. I was busy with all of my activities and work. This kept my mind off of what was to come; Easter was a repeat of

Christmas. I wanted to stay home and I knew mom did to. Frank insisted we honor the invitation for dinner at his sweet hearts house, so we had no choice.

By now I had earned enough to buy mom an electric sewing machine. It was hard for her to use the push peddle one anymore. She was not very happy when I told her that I traded her sewing machine for the new one. I did not stop to think about the sentimentality of what I did. Dad had purchased it for her when she first arrived in Morrison. Even though it hurt her to use it, she had a loving attachment to it. There was no going back on what I had done. What was to be a happy mothers day gift was an unwanted one. I regretted my bad judgment forever. There were a few things I had wanted to get for a long time, but with the wedding coming up in October, I knew we would be moving upstairs and decided to wait. I was working every chance I got. The man that owned the cleaners on the corner of Plum Street needed someone to help out two days a week. He knew I was under age, so I became his niece. He paid in cash since I was not of the legal required working age. The rest of the time was spent at my other jobs.

Betty Ann had been working for a doctor, so our time together was getting limited. We went to the movies every Saturday night. I don't think we missed any Doris Day ones. We thought she was great. Spending a quarter a week was my budget for the week. The first day of school seemed to appear out of nowhere. The summer had just flown by so swiftly. We now were high school big shots; ninth-graders. I guess we enjoyed being wallflowers. For something to do that was free, Betty Ann and I went to the school dances. Since neither one of us belonged to the jet set, we never got asked to dance with the boys; at least not the ones we wanted to. The night was like a segregated dance. The boys stood on one side and the girl huddled on the other wall. Only the couples were assured of a night of dancing. I was not ready or in favor of getting stuck with one pre-grown man. I had several good friends of that gender, but that was as far as I was interested. I had come to Warren hoping to have some fun and make new friends and acquaintances. This I did, but with some trepidations. I never quite seemed to fit into the groove that everyone else did, nor was I ever really completely excpected to. Betty Ann had some of the same thoughts. Perhaps that is why we stayed such good friends and did so much together. Bev's sweetheart thought this to be funny: He wrote in my dragon [the class book], 'When you and Betty Ann get married, let me know.' I interpreted this in a derogative way. When I saw Don, I gave him a piece of my mind. I asked who he thought he was. Just because Bev put up with him did not mean he was a Romeo. What made him think we were so undesirable? When the time came that we were adult enough, we would pursue the man of our dreams; in the meantime, we had to grow up graduate and get jobs. Poor Don; his face got so red. Rose, he said I did not mean it that way; it is just that you and Betty Ann are always together so much. I apologized for my rashness, but reminded don that he could have chosen a better dialog to stay forever in my Dragon.

The wedding was held on October 2nd, 1949. I was asked to be a bride's maid and was obliged to say yes. Her sister was maid of honor. I knew who she was from school because she was one of the majorettes. Again I felt the under dog. I made it through the day, but it was not a fun or very comfortable one for me.

Mom insisted that her and I move upstairs and Frank keep the downstairs. This irritated me to no end. Not only was I concerned about her having to climb those steep steps in her condition; now I had the task of redoing the walls. The paper was tacky and very dirty. The whole place smelled of smoke and sweat. The renters were absolute trash as far as I was concerned. On the plus side, I now had my own bedroom and the attic to hang up the clothes. I got to keep the living room furniture and the dining room and kitchen table as well as the chairs. They were buying all new furniture. Frank deserved the best, but I could not help feeling a bit jealous. Mom and I had done without so much for so long that I felt miffed by this.

I put my heart and soul into removing all the paper. It was a harder task then downstairs was. The plaster was so bad that there was no choice but to wallpaper over it. This worried me since a paperhanger did not come cheap. I was about to tackle it myself. Thank goodness one of our cousins stopped for a visit. After hearing my tale of woe, she offered to help me. She had papered their whole house and assured me it was easy. Since the furniture was blue, mom wanted to use blue colored paper. She liked her flower designs so I let her choose what she liked. My room was going to be painted. The walls were not as bad. I chose a white ceiling and burgundy walls. Frank thought it was horrible. All he did was pick on me for my color choice. This time, it was my turn to be me, not what some one else wanted. I painted moms room pale yellow since it only had one window and on the shady side of the house.

Now, I decided it was time for me to get some furniture. I stopped at the furniture store on the east side of town. I chose two end tables, a coffee table, lamps, and a perfectly small enough rocker for mom. The salesman was anxious for the sale by the way he acted. Then I asked if he could deliver everything. He said yes, but there was a small charge. Now I was ready to negotiate my terms. If I put 20 dollars down would 5 dollars a week be acceptable. There was a long pause. Then he answered,

'We normally do not do this.' But you seem like a sincere person. Do you have a job? When I told him I worked two jobs, he was impressed. I gave him the money, signed the sales slip, and picked up the two end tables. He could not believe that I was walking 20 blocks with them over my head. I told him I would stop for the rest each day until I got everything home. Moms rocker was last. It was a surprise for her. No more dangling legs off of a chair that was not made for a five—foot person. I always fondly called her peanut. So, now to buy my dream: I had seen a radio console over town I wanted very much. It had a radio, and record player that had the best sound to be had. There was storage on two sides for all the records I was dreaming of buying. And it was a handsome piece of furniture. No, I was not going to carry thus home. They delivered it free of charge. Beikarks was the only music store in town. Valerie was one of my classmates. She would tell me when the record I was looking for had come in. I gave up my luxury treats to by my records since my savings had run out. Each week I bought an album that I wanted until I had quite a collection. My cousin Jean Vavala had a huge selection. I used to listen to them whenever I visited her and Aunt Censa. Now I could do so anytime I wanted to. I loved singing along with the artist and did not think anyone could hear me over them. Boy, was I wrong. I found out some of the neighbors would come out on their porches to listen to my concert. After that, I tried not to be so vocal. I felt like a show off. I really was doing it for my own pleasure.

CHAPTER 5

Warren Area High School

Memorial day was looming before me and with it the end of ninth grade and Beaty Jr. High School. How can I explain how I felt. There were both feeling of exhilaration and remorse. I could barely wait to enter that school with the spirals on the other side of the bridge from Beaty. I had so many dreams and plans for my three years there. How can a girl from an isolated village and immigrant parents that tried their best portray what she now felt like. I had entered the threshold of Beaty with the same feelings. How much had I really accomplished? My report cards masked my knowledge. Book smart was not world smart. I felt like an offbeat note in a sonata; never quite fitting in; always a footstep behind the crowd. I had so much to learn. I was determined to climb that mountain before I graduated.

The summer passed me by swiftly. There were so many things I had to do. I helped Frank paint the house. The scrapping was a horrendous job. The sound drove me crazy, but I endured. After over hearing one of the spats he and his wife had, I stayed clear as much as possible. She was not pleased with my generous offering of washing her clothes or anything else I did. I was that d===little sister of yours. Since she worked, I thought I was being nice. How wrong I was.

Margie, as Greta now preferred to be known as, came to visit me. She had taken a job as a nanny for a nice well to do family in White Plains, N.J. This enabled her to have the money she needed to survive and not be a burden to her parents. Gratefully, she still was attending school and planned on graduating there. She had brought her boyfriend with her. I hoped she was not going to be hasty and get into a bad situation just to have her own home. I talked to her about this and gave her my opinion. He was okay, but not a mature person. The next week a letter came; Margie has broken up with him.

Betty Ann and I could hardly wait for school to resume. We had a rather boring summer. Both of us worked. We had little time for much else. but we always took time for a bike ride. Sometimes we would take a lunch with us and spread out along the Allegheny River where some cottages lined the bank area. Told her that this was going to be where the dam would some day be. She blew that off in disbelief. We had heard too much talk and not enough action.

The summer ended with a Labor Day picnic. Frank took us to Twin Lakes for the day. It was a good change from the everyday humdrum of the past eight weeks. As I lay on a blanket, my thoughts went to my next three years and what the future held for me. Mom's health was poor. She had high blood pressure among other problems. I wondered what I could do to help her. Neither of us had health insurance. We had a lot of neglected health problems. With what I earned, I barely could keep my mother and I fed and the bills paid. My job at Betty Lee's helped a little. Never would she dream of asking Frank for a nichol. He just never gave it a thought. I never told him how many times I went hungry just to pay the bills and make sure mom ate; however little that was. I had to beg her to eat moist of the time. I went home determined to do well in my classes and get a good job.

The big day had arrived; our first day at Warren Area High School. We were big shots now; high school girls. Since going to college was out of the question for me, I had chosen all business classes. I made sure my beloved a cappella music class was where I wanted it to be. I had no problem with typing, bookkeeping, or English. Shorthand was another story. Writing in a normal fashion was a trying enough. My penmanship had a lot to be desired. These weird swirls and swiggles did not make sense to me. I could not write fast enough. We were always being timed. I tolerated it till midterm; then scrapped the idea.

I replaced it with business law, the best choice I could have made.

Nick Tomasoni was no stranger to me. He was another Calabresi from the west end. We both understood the meaning of pasta fasole. We now were in class together most of the time. We had a lot of fun picking on one another and stayed friends through out the three years. We now became a divided class. The business students were not as well esteemed as the college bound ones were. Each group became more closely knit with members of their group. SSI got to know more students than at Beaty. Some were good classmate friends; none ever close friends. Nan Perry was always ready to talk to me. Living as far away as she did, we could only see each other in school. I joined traffic cop club. This gave me an opportunity to know everybody better even if that was all it did. Besides, I never got marked late for classes.

Nothing changed much for the next two years. I continued to get honor grades through the entire time. Drama class I found to be a biased situation. The same people get chosen for the parts time after time. It was to be a learning experience for all of us. The chosen ones got the parts, the rest of us got stuck doing the dirty work. Since I disliked study hall, for me this was the better choice. I had the job of prompting anyone that forgot lines. This happened more often than the audience realized. My good memory was put to use.

Graduation

CHAPTER 6

My first real job

June 6th, 1953; graduation; the epitome of my dreams: I was handed my diploma. Tears in my eyes, I promised myself that I would never look back on the bad side of my streets again. I had been offered a scholarship I had to turn down, but on the sunny side I had been offered six different jobs. This spoke for my accomplishments very loudly. Foolishly I had accepted the one with the most pay. Never again were my mother or I going to go hungry or cold because of the lack of money.

None of my training the past three years was needed to [lug and unplug calls. The telephone job was not my cup of tea. I ended up getting an injury on my right hand. A girl I graduated with worked next to me and dropped a heavy plug on it. The company denied this and would not give me any compensation for it. Until I could find another job, I had no choice but to stay. However, I warned the supervisor that I would no longer work on the beep board. This was a new up to date system that connected long distance calls much faster than the conventional one, the next day, I was told to work the beep board. I warned the head operator I would quit at break time if she did not get off of it by then. She did not believe me and tried to put me back on. Lunchtime came and I went to my locker, took off the headphones and walked out the door.

I followed my game plan and walked across the street to the Sylvania business office hoping Chet would be there. He was the personnel manager that had offered me a job after graduation. For a 'piddly nichol' difference, I had declined the offer. He had a smirk on his face as I walked in. He knew what I was there for. I told him what I had done and why. He just chuckled and asked me when I wanted to start; tomorrow of course. He knew Frank well and was glad to have me. I then walked down to visit my cousin Sue so I would not alarm mom in any way. The supervisor tracked me down there demanding I return to work or she would make sure I never got another job. She became silent when I told her I had one and that I informed them of the way I got treated. I never did find out how she found me or they would have some reckoning to account for.

CHAPTER 7

The man of my life

That fall two girls, one I knew from school and her sister asked if I would like to go roller-skating with them. Her sister drove like she was being pursued. I vowed to never get back into that car, even if it meant walking six miles to get home. They knew I could not roller skate and said they would help me. Turns out all they had in mind was to snag a man. I stumbled along, holding on to the railing for a few minutes. Disgusted, I made my way to the benches. I noticed two older guys skating around. The one intrigued me. To my surprise, they both came over to talk to me. Ernie, as he introduced himself, asked me to skate. "I'll help you", he said. I knew then he had seen me making a fool of myself. We gave it a good shot. He finally agreed that we should give it up. He agreed I was not cut out for this sport. We sat and chatted for a while and then went to get us a drink. Sherwood had the same idea and appeared just as Ernie was coming back. He asked if I would give him a chance to teach me. I knew what he was up to and said no thank you. I had already made my choice. After we had our drinks, I convinced Ernie to go skating for a while. He had already offered to drive me home and I accepted. In the meantime, the girls showed up to warn me of older men from Jamestown. Thanking them, I went home with Ernie anyway.

It was love at first sight. Ernie was nine years older than me. Thankfully not 'wet behind the ears', he was handsome with a smile that would melt the northpole. He sure melted my heart. He asked out for the next weekend. When he came to the door, mom about flipped. He was balding in the front, but that was not it. His suit made him look like an old member of the club. Then I got the sermon on the mound from Frank's wife. Just because her sister no longer loved her husband who was much older than her she felt this would happen to us. I just ignored her or I may have said something nasty. I was tired of her trying to dominate my life. After all I had been through, her advice was like a drop of water in the ocean.

After my trying tactfully explain to Ernie that I would prefer that he did not wear that suit because it was the wrong color fir him. He went shopping for a new one. This was a huge improvement over the brown one; he looked so much better that mom gave in to him. Then she became defensive of him. She threatened me to not ride him along and dump him. He was driving down from Jamestown in all sorts of conditions. "I would never do this to anyone". Ernie and I became engaged on Valentine's Day. I invited his family down for a get acquainted dinner. A big pot roast seemed the easiest thing to make for that many people. His brother John was amazed. I think he expected a spaghetti dinner that my mom had cooked. When I came to the table with the lemon pie, Ernie took my hand and said can that hold for a minute. Then he took the ring out of his pocket, slipped it on my finger and asked, "Will you marry me?" Totally stunned, it took me a moment to come to my senses. With tears in my eyes, I gave him a kiss and said "Yes, yes"!

We were married June 4th, 1955 at Holy Redeemer Church. Frank gave me away in marriage. Betty Ann was my maid of honor. We honeymooned in Bermuda and settled in Jamestown. MOM CHOSE TO LIVE WITH FRANK and promised that she would come for short visits now and then. There was no way that she was ready for another big change. She had learned to tolerate her daughter in-law better than I had by now. When we moved to Texas 1967 for our son's health, I broke mom's heart. She passed away July 7th, 1967 from a stroke. Can I ever forgive myself?

Fifty—seven years have passed; he still gives me a kiss every morning. We have three children, four grand children, and three great grand children. I have never had to feel that I did not belong when I was in the arms of my beloved husband. We are still dirt poor, but rich beyond all our dreams with intangible love and beauty of our treasured family.

God's children

We are all God's children, one and all
Created to his distinct design
Some of us are short, some very tall
We come very large or quite small

God took a paintbrush in his hand
Thus choosing his five favorite colors
He gave each of us a special design
With the interior holding a superior network
Of humans who live, love, laugh and cry;
Until the day that comes for us to die.

Why then can we truly justify
Prejudice against one another,
If you take a moment you will find
That no one is different on the inside.

Can we learn to live in harmony?
Would kindness and love be harder to give?
Then hatred, jealousy and greed
Is it possible to live and let live,
For the short time before we say goodbye
In the end, it is God's judgment to reward
Souls that lived by his holy creed

God's blessings to all

Mary Rose Raffaele Scala

Preface to the Kinzua Dam, Morrison and the Kinzua Bridge

All through school, I listened to the tales of the Kinzua Dam. Since no one had ant real idea of the total situation, they were gravely confused by it's necessity. I just listened to everyone and kept my opinions to myself. I already knew why it was necessary to be built. Like good wine, I knew it would take time and patience to materialize.

In ending my story, I hope you enjoy the short documentations of the dam, Morrison, and the Kinzua Bridge. I hope you all can come to visit us very soon. There is nowhere in the world quite like it.

The impregnated birth of the Kinzua Dam

As far back as 1905, there was awareness for the need of flood control on the Alleghany River and it's tributaries. Flood stage was over thirteen and caused six million dollars in damages to Pittsburgh alone in the flood of 1907. For over a hundred years, flooding along the Alleghany was not a concern. However, this flood brought about a commission. Their main purpose was to provide flood protection for Pittsburgh by building seventeen reservoirs along the Alleghany and Monongahela rivers. This was cast aside until 1936. Again, Pittsburgh was one of the biggest' target for flooding this flood caused over one hundred million dollars in damage and several more in property losses. At this time, I was one years—old and too young to remember. Stories told to me much later revealed that Morrison, Kinzua, Corydon and other smaller villages around the area were under water. Warren got its share of the flooding. Likewise, all communities along the Alleghany from New York to Pittsburgh got their big share. However, our damages were minute compared to Pittsburgh. By this time, areas near the Alleghany had become more inhabited, causing more damage with each ensuing flood. The corps of engineers, the most powerful organization relating to flood control, presented a study of flood control that became the beginning of a long road of controversy surrounding the modern day Kinzua Dam. Private businesses and other interested groups that would be affected by this study were pushing for canalizing the Alleghany. Just think, had this idea been made a reality, we now would be able to board a steamboat and travel the canals all the way to the great Mississippi river and on to the new Orleans Marti Gras. However, the need for this no longer existed when pipelines were installed to provide raw gas to the areas. The idea of the dam was shelved during World War II. In 1942, another flood hit and millions more in loses were endured. This was the flood that surrounded our little brown house in Westline and caused a great deal of damage to northwestern Pennsylvania. Because it was wartime, nothing could be done. I was still too young to understand the discussions surrounding this dam, but I knew floods frightened me half to death. If a dam would stop the damage and make this place safer, then please hurry and build it. Believe it or not, there is a 70-page document on this controversy. It seemed that the Seneca's stood to lose about a thousand acres of land, traditions, and burial grounds. However, in 1924, they had become Americans in the Pickering treaty of 1794 between the U.S. government and the Seneca Indians. It stated that the land belonged to the Seneca nation and it would be not be acquired by the U.s. unless the Seneca's chose to sell it, then the U.S. would be allowed to acquire it. As U.S. citizens, we were told Uncle Sam was taking our home by eminent domain and we had no say in the matter. Three years later, in the winter of1944, the flood control act authorized a high dam at Kinzua. Again in 1945 and 1947 more flooding occurred. I cannot help but wonder, if the land the Seneca's owned was affected by these high waters. Perhaps our Native Americans were in the same dangers that we were in, but nothing had ever been mentioned. In the meantime, between 1947 and 1956, there were many hearings on the pros and cons of building a dam. The Seneca's were concerned the dam would destroy their land, sacred burial grounds, and all their beliefs. I, as well as thousands of other people, endured the horror and destruction of the flood of 1947. I experienced the fear of death from it and witnessed the vast expanse of water racing over rivers and land like a demon while taking anything in its path. On the other hand, myself, (along with many of the original people), were saddened by the exodus of our homes and the affect on the fauna and flora. The overwhelming thought of losing what we knew as home was at times unbearable. Many felt that if they refused to move, the dream of building a dam would become history. Instead, it became a nightmare with a golden finish. For them, those of us that were still inhabitants of a small unknown, insignificant village were asked to leave shortly after the flood of 1947. I feel that this was just formal procedure since they knew most of us had left and the rest of us planned to leave shortly,. There was nothing for us to stay for. Without work, no one cared to live [in the woods] without conveniences and drive to the towns for work, shopping or any other commodity that Morrison did not have.

You must understand; Morrison was my birthplace. All I ask in exchange for never being able to see it again, is for it to be remembered. My people had given thirty years or more of their lives to the village. No other community quite matches its history because of this. I have empathy for our American friends, but we also sacrificed in many ways. We were not compensated for our losses and expenses that we incurred during our displacement. We left and paid our own way while others received petty to meager compensation at the army corps discretion of what they thought was fair.

I was, as you know, happy to live in Warren. Most of my relatives were quite satisfied with their present way of life. Still, the high dam was a controversy beyond many peoples comprehension. The flood of 1956 hit. That did it. Its destruction was so severe that the high dam was now considered a reality. My brother almost drowned trying to retrieve my Popeye and Sweet Pea Dolls out of his basement. We never had floodwaters that close. We were a half-mile away from the river in a higher elevation than the warren airport. It always got flooded; the west end was a big lake. Rowboats were all over rescuing people. Can you imagine the destruction that 190 miles of this river was causing? This time Pittsburgh had more than enough. Something had to be done and fast. Again, many people lost their lives.

In 1057, the corps brought condemnation into law. Taking of properties was now legal. The U.S. District Court of New York upheld the rights of the U.S. to take the Indians land by eminent domain. The Indians fought back with a stay of time allotted to remain in possession. They hired an attorney to support an alternate plan. The corps agreed to have a look at it then the Seneca's tried to stop the surveying of the lands needed for the dam. That did not work either. One million dollars was put aside for the first phase of the construction to be used as soon as the courts had made a final decision.

The Seneca were denied the right to have their case reviewed and the Cornplanter lands were purchased. During the 1960 elections, the Indians buttered their bread on both sides and appealed to both parties in a last ditch effort to save their lands. This was the sixth Morgan plan rejected. 4,530,000 was appropriated [it was the green light signal to go ahead with the dam construction]] the ground breaking of the dam on October 22,1960, gave the Indians little chance to appeal. They now turned to their last plan. Money. If they had to give up their lands, at least get the most we can out of Uncle Sam.1000acres, 130 families, and 15 million dollars later, the Indians were relocated near Salamanca; land of the Seneca nation. Pennsylvania no longer had Seneca's living on her lands.

The task of removing all the graves was of the highest concern and was not begun until August 26, 1964. This must have been one of the most grueling, emotional, time-consuming tasks undertaken by the men assigned to it. Margie lost her third son in cradle death and he had to be relocated. She and Hank lived in Corydon; nothing could be done until they found housing. They were given an allotted time and finally settled in Randolph, N.Y. Then baby Jeff was moved again. I'm in the emotional throws of the dam. What crosses my mind is: did they find all the old gravesites in Morrison? Many were very deteriorated and hidden by high growth and land shifts. We came across several on our woods adventures. Paganism caused my relatives to fear this discovery. They feared being haunted by the inhabitants of the graves, but nothing ever materialized that I was aware of.

Whenever we came to visit my family, Frank would brief me on the progress of the dam. We came for a visit and I got brave enough to go see how much progress had been made on this dam. As I got out of the car, at the top of big bend and looked down on what used to be the beautiful village valley of Kinzua, my heart sunk. This was the summer of 1962. All I could see was partial foundations, rock, brick, fallen trees, and tons of debris. Frank was really excited about the dam. He was explaining to us the water boundaries, the new bridge location where the marina was to be and where Morrison would be. He had already purchased a lot from the U.S, and planned on building a camp there. It was two miles from the rim rock area. He also was looking for a fishing boat and canoe. You can take the boy out of the country, but you can't take the country out of the boy. I asked him about the topography of the once familiar land because it was now very confusing to me. Morrison seemed misplaced and worse yet, it was to be totally under water. Boats would now go over my homeland. No one else knew where Morrison was either. It wasn't just Santa Claus that was lost.

The corps merely mentioned that Morrison, Kinzua, Corydon, and several other small hamlets were to be destroyed. Regional papers made no mention of Morrison being included in the dislocation. It was the seventh out of six that got missed. Most of the Morrisonites were passé to all this. They had come to love their new homes and their past evaporated as they crossed the Alleghany Bridge into Warren. The older survivors still had deep memories of their past. I felt a deep devotion to my birthplace and to those that sacrificed their lives to it. Since there is no plaque commemorating Morrison, I shall here to fore write its history and my own commemorative plaque.

I refused to go back to look at the dam construction until it was complete. I went to the dedication September 17, 1966. This 129,000,000—acre expanse of water now became the reality of the Kinzua dam country. I have to admit, I was overwhelming pleased with what I saw. We now have a beautiful lake with an impressive spillway that is set in a valley with beautiful hills surrounding it. There were many inlets also in several locations.

In 1967, we moved to Texas and we lost touch with what was happening. Frank had promised to take me to 'Morrison' on a picnic when he bought a boat. True to his word, he took us on that picnic on our next vacation visit. First we visited his camp in the making, then left for the much talked about marina where he launched his boat for the season. Since we were too many for the size of the boat, two trips were necessary. I offered to wait for the second run, too 'chicken' to face the reality of the circumstances. Nothing looked familiar despite the fact that Frank tried his best to familiarize me with the area. Then he said, "Bobo, we are riding over the houses in Morrison". I felt like we were invading all that the waters held stealth. We went ashore and I spotted the old apple trees. I knew immediately where we were; Avanale's farm; the remains of it. Only the hillside apple trees were there to hold testimony to the farm we visited so many times, going home with our pockets full of apples. I could not resist teasing Frank about how we got the apples. Frank, I said, do you think if we went up there to pick a few apples, Mrs. Avanale will come chase us with her heavenly broom. The apples used to rot on the ground, but she would not let us have them. We were Serrici and she was Sicilian. She had a hate towards us but I never knew why. Mr. Avanale was always nice to us. He would just chuckle whenever he saw us being chased only to return after she went back into the house. We lay out the blankets on the grassy shore and spread out our picnic lunch. Then the swimmers headed into the water. We had a nice day.

There is a brochure by the U.S. Dept. of Agriculture called Morrison trail. In the water, the word Morrison appears. It is now a campground with privies and a picnic area [the same one we visited]. The trail is off of Rte 59 and is shown to be 2.9 miles east of the 'Morrison' bridge and is known as 'Morrison Run'

This should be testimony enough to the village once known as just Morrison, Pa. It could not be forgotten since it was a prime recreational a affording visitors parking, camping, boat ramps, picnic area, and comfort stations. I now know the full meaning of those men's words that had come to tell us that we had to leave. They promised it would be an intricate area. It is more than that. It is the shining star of the Kinzua Dam!

I want to welcome each and every one of you that comes to enjoy my land. All I ask is that you respect it and take a moment to contemplate on what it once stood for. Remember people like you once lived under that deep blue water you are riding your boat over. Enjoy the skiing and swimming and I hope you catch many big fish. This is a great outdoor experience. Please don't desecrate it with trash or destruction of any sort. Take home your memories and come back again to Kinzua country; the land of many fishes'.'

The door with the bullet holes

In the summer of 1999, we had a severe drought. For the first time, the dam went nearly dry. We lost a lot of the water inhabitants. The fish loss was the most severe.

My family had heard enough of what they thought was a 'ha, ha' story whenever I talked about the snake. Our son-in-law, Jim now deceased and sadly missed, and our youngest son, Jeff, rode out to check on the situation and try to find the remains of Morrison. They found that all the remaining foundations were still in tact. They walked up to what used to be the driveway in front of all the houses. Low and behold, house no 4 had all the foundation and the door. It was being held in place by a large rock and a beam. The bullet holes were in clear view. One blamed the other for forgetting the camera.

They then drove to the ranger station to ask for permission to remove the door, the ranger explained to them that by the time all the paper work went through, was filed and returned, the dam would probably be filled again. We got our rain; the dam was full again in two weeks. Jim was a scuba diver from California. He offered to dive for the door. O said, thanks, but no. Let it rest in peace with the rest of Morrison. No more 'ha, ha' stories.

Life's treasure chest

As I gaze in the mirror, reluctantly
A revelation reflects, the glory is gone,
Skin so sallow, eyes blurred and beady
There's no choice but surrendering to father time.

Slowly, you have taken my outer beauty away,
Ever so deep within is a treasure held stealth

As you open the door, an accumulation of wealth,
A lifetime of sorrow and joy combined,
The history of a being who has led a full life.

Takes away my cover, it' of no value,
Cautiously turn the ages to the echo of sonnets.
Strip my exterior as much as you like,
But you cannot take my contents
Carelessly throw them aside
Memories adhere, life's treasures abide.

Mary Rose Raffaele Scala

Morrison; Neilyville

A man by the name of James Morrison from Lycoming County bought the large island at the mouth of Kinzua Creek. He also owned Morrison Island at the mouth if Morrison creek, just a few miles from Warren, Pa. A village, (Morrison, in McKean County), is considered to be named after him. He died in 1840 at the age of 104. From 1790 to 1821, there were so many Morrison families around that it was hard to track them. It was thought, however, that they all were descendants of James Morrison of Warren County.

Logging began to flourish in the northwestern area of Pennsylvania. That created many mills to be built. Chemical plants saw an opportunity to locate there.

In 1884, Joseph Neily from Baltimore, Md., bought 225 acres in Hamilton Township near Red Bridge area, known then as Neilyville. He operated an oar factory in Kinzua and built a second one in 1880 in Neilyville [Morrison]. The mill was located one half mile up Chapel Fork; laying on both sides of the stream. He completed lumbering at this location in 1894.

The land in the areas of Hamilton and Corydon Township belonged to the French. George Ball and James Norton bought a sawmill and three acres from the French and s built at Morrison in the fall of 1891. In May of 1893, Ball purchased 1000 acres that bordered both sides of Hamilton and Corydon Township. He then purchased a small shay and ran the railroad up Morrison Run to its headwaters. It is also said to have crossed Kinzua Creek and ran up to Dutchman run; a distance of one half mile [the C.C.C. consisted of 100 German prisoners later at that location]

Ed Anderson owned 1500 acres of land in the Morrison area that he lumbered for many years. He also purchased a mill and by 1914 built a three-mile railroad up Mud Lick that reached several tracks of his lumbering lands.

Anderson owned a store, a church, a boarding house and several homes in Dunkle. The Henry Anderson family was the first Morrison homesteaders. Desertion and deterioration brought the end to all the buildings at Dunkle with the building of the dam. The camp for social people is all that remains. Dad used to haul trash out for then. I don't recall the buildings; just the pine trees along the road that use to be the C.C.'s area which had been stripped bare of any trees by Anderson.

Logging began to flourish in the northwestern area of Pennsylvania. With this many sawmill were built in the area, with the population flourishing because of the logging industry. Chemical plants saw an opportunity to locate there as well.

Kinzua Valley Chemical Company was one of the last plants to be built by Heims and Bubbs. This was located in Morrison because of its accessibility to natural gas and an abundance of hardwood.

William Wienold had been supervisor with McKean County Chemical Company for eighteen years. After consolidation by

Heims and Bubbs, he was transferred to the Morrison plant and remained there until the plants final days. He passed away, as well as Mrs. Weinold shortly after. He was a hard man to work for with his take it or leave it attitude. He never took any time off except for three days of illness for fear something could go wrong. He was a perfectionist in every way. His plant was cleaner than some I had been in. Compare John Tassone always had a broom in his hand sweeping in between firing the massive furnaces. Things were done Mr. Weinold's way or you found your way to the door. A lot of people did leave. They could not tolerate his arrogant attitude and moved to either Johnsonburg or Beaver Falls, Pa.

Weinold's reward for his faithfulness to the company was $30.00 a week and a large four bedroom, two story house with all the conveniences we didn't have. This included an inside bathroom and electricity. The outside was painted a medium moss green with vanilla cream trim. There were screens on the windows and doors. A crank telephone hung on the large kitchen wall. He had two adult children; Edith and Charles. Charles ended up managing the plant because of his father's illness and remained there till the end. Mr. Weinold was still considered the boss. Edith was a very kind and friendly person. She always had a smile for everyone. Sporting a big cigar in his mouth most of the time, Charlie's greeting was a cool nod. He only spoke to give orders to his Italian immigrant workers. The Morrison guys called him 'lo buffo' meaning bullish. In the exodus of Morrison, Charles and Edith ended up living next door to my friend Dorothy Weaver in Warren.

Wood for the plant operation came from Marshburg [Marsha—burgo], the north branch of Chapel Forks and Indian Run. Also Anderson supplied wood in the teen years of operation. In 1935, the trains ceased operations. The tracks [most of them] were torn down and trucking took over. Pa RR refused to repair the tracks and the truss bridge.

During the trains operating days, my oldest cousins, Carl and Bruno Vavala, Zia's oldest sons, operated the wood train.

They both were engineer, fireman, and brakeman. Later, Loquist and Chuck Ezzolo took the reins until after World War II. Bill Campbell [Campbell run and the snake] and John Sewell were the operators.

It is documented in Tabor's sawmills among the derricks that 40 men were needed to run the plant. However, Tabor was only able to come up with 20 names. My dad, Uncle Rocco, and 18 younger Morrisonite's were omitted from his files for some reason. I do know that dad did lumbering part of the time, but this was an extension of the plant's needs and operations; so did some of the others mentioned. At least two people at a time were assigned to lumbering. It took two people to fell a tree with a straight saw.

Tabor enlightened me on the mysteries of Avonalie's farm(2.9) and the severely deteriorated storefront. Mrs. A. attempted to sell old wormy candy bars to us girls that had been around since the days of Methuselah. We dreaded having to go for eggs when our hens were molting. At one time, it was a spur-market fed off of Andersons store in Dunkle. Two old gas pumps graced the creek side of the road [that was across the road from the store. The store was a large living room turned into a storefront. There was about five feet by eighteen feet long walking space. Shelving and enclosed cases lined both sides. The door to the rear went directly to the kitchen. It was a two story-building witch I assume had at least three bedrooms. Before Avonali took it over as a farm, Mrs. Ezzolo and Mrs. Sambroia managed the store. Which one lived in the house, I do not recall being told; nor do any of the surviving Morrisonite's.

This brings Morrison up to my childhood days. The plant survived through the depression and World War II. All the credit, I am sure was in favor of management. Had Mr. Weinold not gotten such devoted conscientious employees, where would he have been? How many can you fire before no one wants to work for you at all! The old, Italian boys had a sneaky sense of humor about him. He never knew what they were said about him, nor did they ever tattle on each other. They always had a guard 'dog'. Truly, their devotion lay in the knowledge that despite hard times, inconveniences, and kastopo rule, they had it better than many compardi's that came to the wonderful get rich U.S.A. Where else could they work, live off the land and have housing for $5.00 a month?

After the flood, the bridge we crossed before it succumbed to the raging waters was not repaired for some time. Two months after those men gave us the big offer, the plant was junked. That is when we all started to leave. Most of us moved to Warren. A few went to Kane or Johnsonburg.

Weinold ruled for 30 years. My people and neighbors worked with blood, sweat, and tears for this company. It was Heim and Bubbs that reaped the most benefit. Mr. & Mrs. Weinold passed away. They had given their lives to the chemical plant's success. Many factors caused all the failings of all the plants. The need for the products that they produced changed with newer ways to make the end products they had been used for. The only thing that remained in demand was charcoal. I watched my dad, as he stood hunched with a shovel, constantly turning the rows of wood that turned into charcoal. It was a hot dirty job. The chemicals were not known then to be a hazardous or to cause of cancer. I believe that the fumes dad inhaled day after day was a major contribution to his demise. He died from stomach cancer. A man of his intellect deserved better, but times were hard and he endured. Heart attacks were the second malady of the older workers. Gratefully, the younger ones were spared.

So, where is 'Morrisono'? Morrison lies six miles north of Kinzua Dam and approximately 20 miles south of Kane in the heart of the waters. It is a memory to those that still walk this earth. Some have nostalgia for it and others treat it with indifference. They tend to forget how they got to be where they are and who gave up their lives for them.

Morrison to me is my birthplace; my hometown. It's where my mom suffered so many years of discouragement and pain. It's where my dad (who was one of the owners of Timpano Tile Co in the Serre,) had to give up all because of the results of World War I, to come to the U.S. and slave for a pittance. I regret his dreams never came true for him. Frank and I never would have gone back to Italy. We were too rooted in Americanism. I regret that I could not keep my promise to my dad on his deathbed that I would return to Serre and take care of his beloved villa. Because of my age when he died, I was given no authority in this matter. It was sold against my wishes and I suffered a great loss. Only my handicap is keeping from making my promise partially good.

Now, Morrison is a monument to my past, as well as to those that have found their final home. It shall not be forgotten.

Ode to the forgotten village

Oh running waters deep and long
You flow along singing an old song
Deep within your bowels secrets abound
I hear you whisper without making a sound

Steadfast you hold the remains of each home
That a monstrous shovel could not hone
To be carried off to some distant place
Each foundation in mud and rock incased

You listened to the cries of every soul
That was displaced, forever lost
To the land they came to call home.
Never losing their past, for it shone
In every breath of their daily life
Bravely they endured despite the strife.

So, go on, sing your praise and glory
To each spirit that now tells their story
There's someone listening as you hum
Alas, her days blessed, sand not yet done
Morrison will forever live, a monument in time
For those that lived, loved and died in her bosom
sublime.

Maria Rosina Raffaele
[Mary Rose Raffaele Scala]

The Kinzua Bridge

The Kinzua Bridgewas a single track that is 10 feet wide by 2053 feet long. As a six year old, I viewed this 'wonder of the world' with an apprehensiveness that now amazes me. As a child, watching two locomotives and 2000 feet of cars loaded with wood and coal plus a caboose as it was crossing in front of me, I became terrified. I made dad promise me that he would  never go on that road to hell. Dad told me not to worry; it had been there a long time; almost sixty years. That is a lot of coal, oil, and wood being transported across those tracks in the sky.

Originally, when the bridge was built it took 40 men in 1899 to build it with steel. It rested on patented hollow iron steel tubes they called phoenix columns that were inserted into quarried rock from the area hillsides. It was a single track 10 feet wide x 2053 long and 300 feet deep in its deepest concave that tower was 198 feet in length. It had a total of 20 towers and was designed to support 266 shot tons at a cost of $167,000; a bargain for 2009's $8.7 million comparative.

Trains were restricted to 5 miles an hour because locomotives and wind caused the bridge to shift and vibrate. This I witnessed quite clearly on a windy April day in 1947.

In1888, the N.Y.P.E.E.W. went bankrupt and merged with the Erie railroad and they became the owners of the bridge. By March of 1900, the last train crossed the iron bridge. The locomotives now weighed 85 percent more than the previous ones and the iron bridge was not steady enough to handle its weight and that of the coal and wood laden cars.

Ten days later, work began to re-construct the bridge of iron. It took approximately 100 men working 10 hours a day for four months to rebuild it. It was re-opened around Labor Day. September 6, 1900 and was to 'safely' accommodate the largest steam loco's in the world, the 511 Shock Ton. The cost for this replacement was placed at &295,000. However, Grimm who designed the span, felt it was a big savings to re-use the old tasp bolts and even re-treaded the sleeves on them. This was later documented as a major role in the bridges demise.

The Erie Railroad obtained passage on the nearby B & E line in 1950, thereby bypassing the aging bridge, it was still deemed unsafe for heavy use and by 1963 Governor Scranton formed the Kinzua Bridge State Park that opened in 1970. In 1977, the bridge was put in the national register of historic railroads.

During this time, the bridge had been sold to Covalchic; a salvage company. Upon seeing the bridge, Nick could not bear to dismantle it. To him, it was a rare gem. He purchased all the land around the bridge and formed the Kinzua Bridge State

Park.(6.1) That included about 316 acres of beautiful wooden land. He instated excursions from Kane to the bridge and back. Later they were extended from Marionville to the bridge and on to Kane and back.

In 2002, inspections failed due to invasive rusty steel in several places. It was closed on August 2nd of that year. Engineers, at that time stated that a high wind [very common and constant there] could shift the center of gravity causing uneven weight and the bridge would be found in the hellhole of Kinzua Creek.

February 2nd, 1903, M. Brode and Co., a national leader in railroad restoration began repairs on the bridge. July 21,1903 at 3:15 p.m. a tornado with winds of up to 112 miles an hour struck the sides of the bridge. Eleven towers were torn away from their concrete bases. The center of the bridge to the farther end lay resting in the Kinzua Creek valley bed. [My vision as a six year old. Only more of the bridge was involved in my vision.] Fortunately none of the men were injured. Then they continued to stabilize the remaining bridge. Why behooves me was e the popular opinion was to attempt to rebuild it. Some people never learn when to call it quits.

We, here in Kinzua Country are blessed with some of the most beautiful breath taking land in the world,. The park has various types of trees, shrubs, and flowers. In June the mountain laurel with its delicate pink clusters of blooms sand and euphoria of scents for miles around. Wild flowers flourish along the pathways and in the wooded area. From early violets to late blooming lilies it is a colorful, awesome sight. I had the privilege of picking these gems from March through October as a little girl. I was always careful to not hurt the 'mommy plant'. You, the welcomed visitors, are invited to thoroughly enjoy them, take pictures of as many as you wish, but picking is prohibited in state parks in Pennsylvania. You will be able to enjoy picnic areas, rest stops, comfort stations, and upon arriving at the permitted area of the remaining bridge, there are two spot scopes from an observatory for your use. (2.12)

When you have fulfilled all your desires of this one if a kind area, the Kinzua Dam is not far and should be made a must on your itinerary.

Included in this document you will find photos our son, Jeff Scala, took. He had taken our cousin Kate Raffaele from Sydney, Australia on what was to be one of the last excursions allowed across the span. Kate was in absolute awe by it all. Nothing in Australia came close to this beautiful scenery she experienced in our Kinzua country, not even the Black Mountains.

I reluctantly agreed to let them go, but quite frankly I was a nervous wreck all the while they were gone and prayed all would go well. Did my father's power of healing come with this telepathy I so often experienced, and became a reality too many times? It sounds farfetched and scary, but I am told that it is a gift from above.

The Dedication

I n loving memory: of my parents Bruno and Raffaela; My brother Frank and all the Morrisonites; relatives and friends who have reached their final destinations. Also, in loving memory of our beloved son-in-law we lost tragically and will forever miss. Last but not least my dear friend Margie [Greta] who reached her final resting place March 13th, 1908; a day before my birthday.

Acknowledgement

I wish to express my deepest gratitude to the Warren Public Library, Pennsylvania Dept. of Forestry, Kinzua Visitors' Buereau, The Westline Inn, and the Smethport Historical Society for providing me with documentations on the various regions of Kinzua country. I thank Fred Adams for providing the wonderful pictures from Serra San Bruno and Al Kondak for the copy of his illustration of my alm mater, Warren Area High School.

Also: my love and gratitude to my family and friends for their support and assistance in preparing my story for publication. A special thank you to Jeff, who patiently endured my inexperienced use of a computer, researched material, scanned photos and cooked meals while I pecked at the keys.

Gratitude

A special remembrance: to a lifetime friend who has sustained us in so many ways. The only thing Nick Tomassoni knows is kindness, giving, and understanding. Angels like him do not come cheap and are not born everyday. Thank you, compare, for everything. May God bless you and keep you. We thank you from the bottom of our hearts.

The Scala family

E finutu chow sempre belli gorni.

Bibliography

Photos; unless otherwise state dm, family possession
Poetry; entirely the works of the author, Mary Rose Raffaele Scala

Sawmills Among The Derricks by Thomas T. Tabor III: Book No. 7: Logging Railroad Era of Lumbering Pennsylvania Pg.: 725,726,727,730,732,736,738. The Westline Gazette—Westline Inn Today;

Departure of the Valley Railroad
Front page.

Kinzua Dam; Wikipedia;
        Front page
Ancestry. Com; Passenger List 1820-1957
        1940 Census Results
The Kinzua Dam: Progress or Perfidy
        By George H. Moeller
        Pg. 2-24
Knox, Kane, Kinzua Railroad Pamphlet

Purpose of My Story

I have often wondered how many other persons experienced a childhood such as I did with all the bizarre situations that occurred. I am certain that there will be a cause for doubt and skepticism when people read about it. However, they are all true. I don't wish to repeat any of them.

Ultimately, I felt Morrison held a unique story of immigrants (mostly related) that held steadfast to their heritage; yet survived by the gifts of the land along with all the challenges and hardships.

I also wanted to share in the beauty of Kinzua Country and the Dam that caused us to say goodbye to our homes forever. Kinzua was a quaint village set in a beautiful valley. Morrison (a minute village just a short six miles away) was forgotten in the demise of it. Now a prominent boating and outing area; it is known just for that; not for what it embraced before it was blanketed with the cool waters of the dam.

Photo Index

2.52 Walking along the road through Morrison.

2.6 Queeny sneaking off up into the hills to chase rabbits. The boarded up schoolhouse is in the background.

2.7 Dad with our 28-inch brown trout.

2.8 Morrison's twenty-ton Heisler used to transport lumber to the chemical plant.

2.9 Apple anyone? The apple orchard is presently known as Morrison Trail. The house and barn (what's left) sit in the water on the left hand side of the picture.

2.10 Cousin Neddy and the 'T' in front of our house.

2.11 Our famous transportation to and from Ludlow; also, our caring driver

2.12 Jeff Zaffino: Morrison's guardian.

2.13 Morrison Hiking Trail. My old stomping grounds.

2.14 Ludlow's last year; my fifth and sixth grade classmates.

Westline

3.1 Shirley and I. Swing Frank made me in Westline.

3.2 Our house surrounded by flood waters. Westline, 1942

3.3 Frank taking a break from the pig.

3.4 The Westline Inn; it is now a nice place to stay over and has an excellent restaurant.

Lewis Run

3.4 My first best lifetime friend; Greta (Margie).

3.5 Lewis Run 'Angels' First Holy Communion. Me; top of my head; back row, third from left.

3.6 Frank: The "famous" spaghetti cowboy with his prize western guitar.

3.7 Uncle Shorty dressed up to go nowhere. Roads were all flooded.

3.8 Isolated cabin surrounded by water.

3.9 'Preview' of the future dam. Water was everywhere. Bye, bye, bridge.

Kinzua Dam

4.1 Map.

4.2 Gates of the Kinzua Dam in winter taken before 9/11. It is now off limits.

Warren

5.1 Betty Ann Simko and me on the platform of the Joseph Warren Memorial.

5.2 Illustrated by Al Kondak. Thank you, Al.

> Warren Area High School; Alma Mater
> High in the air thy spires are towing,
> Gleaming in the light;
> Sons and daughters bound by duty,
> Give their love to you.
> While the solemn shades embowering,
> Wave the blue and white.
> Feeling in its' tranquility,
> Wave the blue and white.

5.3 Our Wedding Ceremony in progress inside the beautiful, breath-taking interior of Holy Redeemer Church.

Kinzua Bridge

6.1 Cousin Kate in awe and disbelief of the Kinzua Bridge and scenery. It was to be the last trip the tour train made. The bridge was forbidden to be usded again. A tornado blew half of it down later on and they rebuilt what was left into a tourist attraction.

Cover Design and Photo Restoration by Goffredo della Scala Studio